Sophie Kasiki: In the Shadc

First Draft Publishing/*Primary*

Sophie Kasiki: In the Shadow of Daesh
Liz Harris: Foreword and translation

First published in French by Robert Laffront,
Paris, 2016. (A) Édition Robert Laffront, S.A.,
Paris, 2016.

First published in English in Germany 2021
by First Draft publishing GmbH © Sophie Kasiki

Foreword: © Liz Harris
Translation and Editor: © Liz Harris

978-3-944214-34-4 *(softcover)*
978-3-944214-33-7 *(kindle)*
978-3-944214-32-0 *(epub)*

The cover photo shows a street in Raqqa, Syria 2018
Cover Photography: © Anand Gopal
Typefaces: Heimat Mono *www.atlasfonts.com* & Arnhem
www.ourtype.be

ww.firstdraft-publishing.com
info@firstdraft-publishing.com

Table of Contents

Liz Harris:
Foreword

In January 2015, Sophie Kasiki quietly resigned from her job, telling no one in her family. A month later, she caught a flight to Istanbul with her four-year-old son on the pretext that she was going to volunteer in a Turkish orphanage. Two days later she was in Raqqa, capital of the so-called "Islamic State." She left behind a stable home, a good job, a loving family and a loyal husband to live in a city under the control of violent, religious extremists in a country at war. Sophie was one of the lucky ones; once the reality of life in the "Caliphate" sunk in, she managed to escape. This book is her attempt to unravel the spaghetti-like tangle of motivations that led her to set foot on a path which could easily have resulted in her death, or a long, miserable exile in the detention camps of northern Iraq. It was also intended as a warning to others who might find themselves lured down the same road.

Since the Russian invasion of Afghanistan in 1979, foreigners have flowed to, and between, conflicts in the Muslim world; Kashmir, Bosnia, Chechnya, Somalia, Iraq. While some brought their wives and families in tow, most of them were men. The Islamic State of Iraq and Syria (ISIS) stands out both for the sheer numbers and global diversity of its foreign recruits, and because so many women flocked to join them. Over forty thousand people from 80 countries gravitated to the ISIS-controlled area that spanned Iraq and

Syria, including nearly six thousand from Western Europe.[1] A thousand of these Europeans were women. Some women had followed their husbands. Others were enticed there by women who had already made the journey, such as the notorious Glaswegian Muslim convert Umm Layth, with the promise of an exciting, meaningful life and marriage to a dashing *jihadi* groom. Still more were wooed online by ISIS men themselves. While the women of ISIS did not take part in active combat, some took on substantive roles to help the organisation maintain its grip on local people and adherents alike, such as those who joined the *Al-Khansaa Brigade*, the much feared all-female religious enforcement unit.

The motivations underlying the choice to leave one's family, friends and country for an uncertain future in a war zone has pre-occupied academics and policy makers for decades. Efforts intensified following the US-led invasion of Afghanistan in 2001, when foreign fighters joined the Taliban to fight against the countries in which they were born and raised.

The mid-2000s saw a narrative develop within counter-extremism circles to explain the phenomenon. When immigrants from South Asia, Africa and the Caribbean came to the UK in large numbers during the 1950s and 1960s, they were greeted by racism and discrimination. This first generation of migrants gritted their teeth, dug in, worked hard and raised families. Their children were brought up in Britain, yet endured the same racism as their parents. At best, they faced constant questions about where they were "really" from, at worst told to "get back" there. Yet when they visited their parents' homelands for holidays, they realised they didn't there fit either. So who were they? What were they? For some, radical Islam would fill the identity vacuum, while poverty, inadequate education and a lack of opportunity

---

1   Cook, Joana and Vale, Gina. *From Daesh to 'Diaspora': Tracing the Women and Minors of Islamic State.* London. International Centre for the Study of Radicalisation, 2018.

exacerbated the situation, creating fertile ground for extremist recruiters. Since early 2000s, millions have been spent on counter-radicalisation programmes in the UK and throughout Europe, targeting "vulnerable" youth to persuade them the world was not a binary choice between Islam and the West, with its foreign policy that seemed to place "Muslim lands" permanently within its sights.

Sophie's story does not fit with this narrative of alienation, and although money was tight in her childhood, she does not claim to have been disadvantaged. Neither was she following a man; whenever I begin telling her story, listeners almost invariably chip in with assumptions that she was a "jihadi bride" or that she was coerced by her husband, whom they assume to be Muslim. In fact, Sophie remains married to an atheist schoolteacher, a white, middle-class French man. While she moved to France from Cameroon at the age of nine, she makes no mention of racism in her experience of her adopted country, or of feeling alienated as a citizen. She was well-educated, with a meaningful profession as a special needs support worker and even worked on social cohesion projects, encouraging other less integrated immigrants to embrace French culture.

While she converted to Islam from Catholicism, she states this was a deeply personal, spiritual journey. In her own words, there was no "charismatic preacher" who turned her head. It's arguable (from what she tells us) whether she was "radicalised" at all; she had only a passing interest in politics and does not profess chauvinistic views about Islam. So what on earth possessed her?

Sophie digs deep in her past to answer this question. She is unflinching in her self-examination and while moving, her account is devoid of self-pity. The reasons she unearths are compelling. Her search, it seems, was for that elusive quality which drives men and women to take all manner of seemingly illogical decisions: *meaning*. The sense that there had to be something else, something out there, a noble cause to which she could devote herself that went beyond

what she could achieve at home. Sophie's desire for meaning was, it seems, borne from the depression that haunted
her since a traumatic event in her early life; being needed
helped dispel it. Combined with difficulties in her personal
life she was a prime target for the men who recruited her,
men she had known through her community work in France
and who knew exactly which buttons to push.

Sophie's story chimed with me, as my own need for
meaning led me to a career in humanitarian aid. It led me
away from home comforts, from relationships, from my
family, from my friends. On occasion, it led me into situations of great danger. For years I worked in prisons in the
conflict zones of Indian Kashmir and Afghanistan, inspect-
ing the treatment of people known variously as prisoners-
of-war, security detainees, terrorists or militants, in order to
ascertain whether they were being held in accordance with
the international laws that protected them from torture,
summary execution and other privations. In both conflicts
I noticed the difference between the local fighters and their
foreign counterparts. While the locals sought to wrest control from existing governments for the gain of their own
communities, the foreign fighters I met had were motivated
by idealism, to fight the good fight on the part of – what
they believed – to be an oppressed minority. Some were
zealots, others were orphans, college drop-outs and former
drug addicts. It wasn't unusual for them to ask me whether
they could get a job with my organisation – or one like it –
when they were released. They were looking for meaning
too, it seemed. Years later I became a recruiter for my organisation, travelling the world to find candidates to fight for
our particular cause. Perhaps if I'd met Sophie on one of my
trips to France, her trajectory might have been different.
Her motivation – and other parts of her history – was not so
different from my own, and this is one reason I translated
her book.

The other was a conspicuous gap in the literature. There
are tens, if not hundreds of books on the Islamic State.

Analyses by academics, examining its origins, strategy, tactics and philosophy. Accounts of mercenaries, who joined the Kurdish *peshmerga* in order to fight them. The testimonies of Yazidi women, torn from their families and sold as slaves for the enjoyment of ISIS cadres. There are books by ex-hostages whose countries paid for their freedom and journalists who sneaked into ISIS-controlled territories to report on life behind the black flag. Yet first person accounts of those who joined IS from the West and then escaped are sparse; there are books *about* them, but I have found only two books written by returnees in their own words, of which this is one. Both were in French, the authors from Belgium and France respectively. To date, no British returnee has published their account.

This is understandable. Those who returned home to the UK disillusioned with ISIS have little incentive to speak out. It would bring them to the attention of the security services, if they were not already on the radar. They would face the ire of their own communities and of the public at large. They may fear a prison sentence, if they have not served one already. They may have well-founded fears of having their citizenship stripped and of deportation to countries they barely know, due to a change in the law in 2014 which allows deprivation of citizenship even where it might cause statelessness.[2] Finally, they may have valid concerns of retaliation from ISIS, even in the UK.

Yet as society, we can learn valuable lessons from the testimonies of those who do things we find inexplicable. This does not equate to condoning their actions, but it may help us find new ways to prevent them. Broader public insight may also help encourage tolerance, both for repentant returnees and those desperate to come home. Finally, accounts such as Sophie's have the credibility to reach those who may find themselves courted by extremists in the future. This is especially pertinent for women and girls; out of 1,765 Western Europeans who made it back, only 138

---

2   Section 40 (4A) of the Immigration Act, 2014.

have been women. The Syrian war may have drawn them in greater number than previous conflicts, but they have been the last to leave.

Acknowledgments

Early in 2016, I was browsing the internet when I came across Sophie Kasiki's story in the Guardian. Her book had just been published and she'd given a rare interview to a journalist. A further search brought up a rather more lurid story in the Daily Mail. I was intrigued; like many, I had been transfixed by the rise of the Islamic State, horrified by their violence and perplexed at why anyone would want to join their ranks. I bought the book immediately and read it over a weekend. By the time I finished, I knew I wanted to translate it into English as I felt it made an essential contribution to the existing literature on this subject. I had never worked as a translator, let alone translated a book before. In fact, I had only started learning French four years earlier and was almost entirely self-taught. But the language would prove to be the easiest part of the task; the greatest challenge was working out how to get a book published in the first place. I had no knowledge of the publishing industry or any contacts within it. In all respects, I was starting from zero.

It is said it takes a village to raise a child; the same claim can be made for translating and publishing a book. So many people have helped and encouraged me along the way that it would be impossible to name them all, but I thank everyone who humoured me during this escapade. Above all, I am indebted to my network of linguist friends scattered around the world, to Lucy Metcalfe, Bronia Kupczyk, Ahmed El Khamloussy, Arturo Rago and Leila Kherbiche, who helped me at the drop of a text, despite their busy lives, when I was stuck on a sentence, baffled by an idiom or attempting to unpick a reference to French, African or Middle Eastern culture. I could not have managed without your help.

It is often not understood outside linguist circles that while solid knowledge of the source language is essential, a fine translation owes itself to the mastery of one's mother tongue. I cannot say the extent to which I have achieved this goal, but I would like to thank Myra MacDonald, Jon Hemming and Praveen Swami, along with the students and staff from my MA course in creative nonfiction at the University of East Anglia, for their invaluable feedback on my writing.

Staying motivated was also a challenge at times, not least because this project was unfunded and carried out in my spare time. Andy urged me to keep going at a critical moment when I considered abandoning it. Christine and Sol, my big sister and brother-in-law, were simply always there for me, and I am grateful to my friends Kate, Alfredo, Olly, Anna, Kylie, Meira, and Esther for each keeping me on track. A special mention to Jess, as a fellow SOAS graduate, linguist and aid worker, who inspired me when I had all but buried my dreams of writing. Thanks also to Chris S, both for his belief in the book as an expert on the subject, and for taking me for dinner the evening I finished.

The process of bringing a foreign language book to market takes time. One must find a publisher willing to negotiate the rights and pay for them. Events in my personal life and the Covid pandemic further delayed the project. I am deeply grateful to Alex Strick and Felix Kuehn at First Draft Publishing for taking me on and for their patience, advice and friendship over the years.

Translating a book is hard, but without an author there would be no book at all. I am thankful to Sophie Kasiki for having the courage to write her story and Pauline Guena for helping her. Sophie and I have never met or corresponded directly, but her swift replies through Pauline to any queries I had about the text were much appreciated. Thank you, Sophie. I hope we meet one day.

Finally, I must thank my parents, who raised me to be curious about the world and to follow my heart. I would not be here without them.

The Dust of War

The road stretches out in front of us like a dirty yellow ribbon, winding through the devastated plain. Here and there, a few miserable looking farms are dotted between deep craters gouged from the earth by Bashar al-Assad's bombs. Some still show signs of life, yet you don't see a soul. Never. Those who remain keep themselves hidden.

Ridges of mud and stone protrude like twisted lips around the gaping holes in the ground. The land has been contorted by violence, gnawed away by the war that has been devouring it for the past five years. I'm speeding through this desolation, my son asleep in my lap beneath my niqab. With one hand I clasp his warm, heavy body against me. With the other, I cling with all my strength to the skinny frame of a man who was a stranger yesterday, but upon whom our lives depend today.

Malik. Our saviour.

The motorbike races onwards, as fast as its weary engine will allow. I can hardly breathe as the wind flattens my veil against my nose and mouth. Every minute of every hour since we escaped counts towards our survival. They are searching for us in Raqqa. Hunting us down. When they realise I've escaped from the city, this is where they'll come to look – the road leading to the Turkish border.

Malik swerves to avoid the potholes and bumps which warp the dusty asphalt. I'm riding side-saddle unsteadily behind him, tangled up in my burqa, now coated with the same inescapable yellow dust that shrouds everything around us as far as the eye can see.

Mud splattered pick-up trucks hurtle past us from the other direction, horns blaring, their swaying cargo of young men bunched together around 12.7 mounted machine guns. They're clad in mismatched army camouflage, hair and beards flowing, moustaches trimmed, Kalashnikovs slung across their backs pointing to the sky. As they pass us their fists fly upwards, faces fierce with pride. They're known as *mujaheddin* here, these young men from all over the world. Across the border they're called *jihadists*.

The army of Daesh, going into battle.

Our route has been meticulously planned to avoid checkpoints – they'd know instantly that I'm not Malik's wife. They'd only need to lift my veil and see my face, or ask me a question in Arabic and realise I don't speak a word. For me, that will mean death by stoning. For Malik, torture then beheading. My son will disappear forever into an Islamic State orphanage.

We hit a bump, Malik slams on the brakes and we skid across the tarmac. He accelerates, deftly wrestles the bike round and we're on the way again. I tighten my grip on Hugo, my shoulder numb from the weight of his head. There are two men from the Syrian Free Army in a car in front of us scanning the road for surprise roadblocks set up to catch people like us. Another car carrying armed men brings up the rear. They'll use those weapons if we're stopped.

Despite the fear, exhaustion and discomfort, my eyes grow heavy and my head sinks onto Malik's back. But there's no escape from the question that goes round and round my head. How on earth did I get here? How have I ended up fleeing for my life in a war zone, my son asleep in my arms, our lives in the hands of strangers?

I'll ask myself this question over and over again in the months to come. They'll certainly be plenty of time to think. I'll face repeated interrogations from my husband and family – not to mention the police. Upset, horrified and incredulous, all of them will insist on answers.

I'll try. I'll seek out all possible sources of the tsunami that swept up my life over the past year, dragging my loved ones into its wake and putting my son and me in mortal danger. I'll dig deep into my past, into my childhood and youth, to try and unearth the roots of the unhappiness that led me to become so deluded. I'll wrack my brains trying to pinpoint where I went so wrong.

Everyone has their own path in life. Mine led me to the Islamic State with my four-year-old son on the cusp of my 33rd birthday.

Yet there's no one event in my life that can explain it. To assume religion as the sole cause would be a mistake. Yes, I converted to Islam and was what is known as a 'new convert'. It's also true that I'd embraced the religion enthusiastically. But it would be inaccurate and lazy to claim that this is the reason I went.

Try as I might, I simply can't find an obvious explanation for the events that unfolded last February.

1: A Childhood

I was born in 1981 in Yaoundé, Cameroon and for the first nine years of my life I lived in a blissful bubble of happiness.

My mother was a tiny woman, as slight as a bird, with a heart of gold. She was head nurse in a free clinic, run by Belgians, and her entire life was dedicated to caring for others. She looked after her mother and her younger sisters, as well as helping her uncles and cousins. But my mother never showed any sign of being tired; she took everything in her stride, as graceful as a swan. She had a radiant smile, which shone even brighter when her eyes rested on me. I don't know if it was because I was the youngest, but I was the apple of her eye – and she was the centre of my universe.

We lived in a big house where I was surrounded by beautiful, independent women, living as they wished. My mother and aunts earned enough for us to live comfortably; our home was well furnished, we wore pretty dresses and there was always plenty to eat. We wanted for nothing. We always spoke French at home as the adults wanted to make sure we children mastered the language.

I never felt I'd missed out by not having a father; my mother was enough for me. My aunts told me he'd been a high-ranking officer in the naval police and had died when I was two or three years old. I had no memory of him, just images in my mind formed from stories I'd heard; he existed only in the words of others. As for friends, I know I had some from the school where my aunt worked, but I don't remember much about them. Happiness for me was playing in our backyard and waiting for my mother to come home. From the moment she came back from work, I wouldn't let her out of my sight. She was so slender that, even as a child, I could wrap my arms right around her body without straining myself in the slightest. Her scent and the memory of her smile is all I have left of her.

Nobody told me my mother was ill. I only understood when I saw her lying on her bed, unable to move. That was a few weeks before the end and she could barely lift the sheet that was draped over her by then. My aunts, sisters and the maids hustled me out of the room. "Go and play outside," was all anyone said to me. I did what they said. This was the African way of doing things. Children didn't ask questions, and no one explained what went on in the adult world to them. I went and played in the courtyard. My mother was dead.

The house was crammed with people. Family from other parts of the country and other countries of the world, including France, where some had settled. My big sister Alice had come too. I hadn't seen her for a long time. Gasping with sobs, she held me tight against her hard, round, pregnant belly; she was expecting her second child. I didn't cry at all, because no one had explained to me what was going on. The house continued to fill with mourners; extended family, neighbours, friends, my mother's colleagues, people she'd cared for, people she'd helped. My uncles were there too, my mother's and my father's brothers. They also hugged me, weeping, before telling me to, go and play with the other children. No one said the words, "your mother is dead" to me, and I wasn't sure if I understood what was happening. Obediently, I went into the yard. But I didn't play. Instead, I sat down on the ground until someone came and scolded me for getting my dress dirty. So I got up and tiptoed past the adults to the room I shared with my cousins. On the way, I noticed that the door to my mother's room was ajar and peeked inside. She wasn't there. The bed had been made and the shutters were closed.

The memory of my mother's Mass is mixed up with all the other masses of my childhood, which are *nothing* like those in Paris or any other French town. In Africa, men and women – but especially women – dress up to the nines when they go to church, and they certainly don't pray in respectful silence. Forget whispering "amen" in hushed tones – they belt it out at the tops of their voices. The air resounds with joyous gospel songs rather than sombre hymns, even during a funeral. Particularly during a funeral, in fact. As the voices of the congregation merged with the music, it was hard to tell where the singing ended and the wailing began. Squeezed between family members in the midst of this tumult, I was completely still.

My future was decided that night. I was to be sent to Paris to live with my sister and her husband. The days blurred into weeks and I spent my time as I always had done; yet I was in limbo, suspended between the end of my old life and the beginning of the one to come. It was autumn and the court-yard was strewn with seedpods from the *siris* trees that no one had swept up. I wandered barefoot through the house, trying not to step on the lines between the tiles on the living room floor. It was my game and I made up the rules. I heard the murmur of lowered adult voices, but nobody noticed me.

I don't know who packed my case; it must have been my aunts, I suppose. Alice had already left for France, where her husband and eldest child were waiting for her. My older sister, not yet even 25 years old, was about to inherit a nine-year-old girl, insensible with grief. Not exactly a gift. I walked away from my bedroom, my country, and my universe. Everything disappeared with my mother. In front of me, there was nothing but emptiness – and fear.

It was my first time in an airplane. When I arrived in Paris, I found my sister and Serge, her husband, waiting for me at the airport with their son. Serge was a tall man, calm and serious. I soon learnt that he was capable of going for

days without speaking. He liked to come home to a quiet
house after a hard day's work and to watch television with
his wife, when the children had gone to bed. He hadn't
asked to adopt a withdrawn, wary little girl. He wasn't particularly interested in understanding what made people
tick, nor was he at ease with flowery language and displays
of emotion. But he became my rock, taking me into his
family without question, for better or worse. My new life
could begin.

Everything was different; the Paris ring road glistening
with rain, the steel grey sky, the traffic jams, the white faces,
the hurried footsteps, the smells and sounds of the city.
Today it seems clear to me I had what is known as childhood
depression. But it wasn't diagnosed at the time and no one
in my family would have dreamed of asking for professional
help for me to get over my grief.

The colour had drained from the world. I'd lost Africa and
my mother's love. I had nothing left and felt worthless – an
unfair burden on my sister and her husband, Uncle Serge,
who'd been obliged to take on an extra mouth when they
were raising their own family and finding it hard enough as
it was. The Paris apartment was too small for all of us and
they couldn't afford anything bigger in the city, so we moved
to a suburb in the small town of Yvelines. I shared a room
with my nephews, where I spent as much time as possible.
I went to school without complaint, but as soon as it was
home time I'd come straight back and curl up in a ball on
my bed. Nobody loves me, nobody *really* loves me, I told
myself, despite Alice's patient efforts.

It didn't occur to me that she was feeling the same pain.
I felt alone and that I no longer served any purpose. Gone
forever were those shining brown eyes, which used to gaze at
me with such love that I'd feel warm from head to toe. My
mother lived only for me. Now she was dead I felt as though
I was good for nothing.

A child's depression is hard to comprehend. I didn't have
the words to describe my feelings and my sister was at a loss

for what to do. So she focused on my outward symptoms. She was anxious when I didn't eat, put me to bed at the same time every night – not too late – and allowed me to leave the light on all night because I was afraid of the dark. I was clean and well turned out, always on time for school, my schoolbag packed and my pencil case stocked with everything I needed. Alice was never late to pick me up. She did her best, yet I shut myself off from her in silence and solitude.

When I stared up at the square patch of sky framed by the window in my room it seemed washed out, lacking the vivid glow of the one I'd left behind. I couldn't reconcile myself to this new sky, heavy with clouds, nor to the cold, blue light and the interminable shades of grey. From the other side of the door I'd hear the hubbub of my sister's family, which I was unable to think of as my own. I'd listen to my little nephew babbling, the baby gurgling, the low voice of my uncle and my sister's laughter. They were good together. They didn't need me.

I'd been yanked from my roots and nothing was the same in this brutal, new reality. Something shifted inside me and I felt detached from the world, as if nothing could really touch me anymore. Parisian chestnut trees, their branches bare for almost half the year, had replaced the flame trees of my childhood. The buildings were grey and dirty, so much taller than my old home. Gone were the ribbons and frills of the weekend Mass and in their place, padded jackets and overcoats. Even the silence was not the same, the relentless drone of traffic forever in the background.

But I was indifferent to it all. Everyone thought I'd adapted easily because I didn't seem bothered about anything. My sorrow protected me from the world; I wrapped myself up in it like a blanket, which I never took off. I spent hours on end drawing on my memories, trying to live in my past. But despite my efforts, I started to forget. I forgot the house, the high steps to the door and the black, cast iron handrail, cold under the palm of my hand. I forgot the smell of my mother's *pondu* – the porridge of cassava leaves and vegetables, or mango. I forgot my aunt's face, the flowers on my favourite sheets and the rainbow that would appear on the bathroom tiles when I washed myself. Everything was vanishing: my cousins' voices in the yard, the lizard crawling along the wall blinded by the sun, my mother's laughter.

My past had disappeared.

At school, I was an average student. Calm, disciplined and somewhat in world of my own, I kept myself to myself and didn't take much notice of the other children. At least no one picked on me. The days passed, with little to distinguish one from the next. Adolescence arrived, but nothing changed. I continued to shut out the rest of the world, coming straight home from school and turning down any invites from my classmates. I had no taste for life.

My nieces saved me. I was 17 years old and my sister was pregnant again, expecting twins. We were going to be even more squeezed and I can't say I was overjoyed. But when I visited Alice the day after the birth and saw the tiny girls nestled together, asleep in the transparent incubators, an intense emotion came over me. I was unable to say a word.

Alice was exhausted, but happy. One of the babies started to mewl like a kitten, sucking in her sleep, hungry but not totally awake.

'Can you give her to me?' My sister asked.

I picked up the newborn as if she was made of glass. I was used to holding babies, but this time I was overwhelmed. She was so fragile and yet so full of life. Snug in my arms, depending on me alone, trusting and oblivious at the same time. Something inside me changed at that moment.

I became a little mother. When my sister carried one of them in a sling on her back, I'd take the other. When she fed one, I looked after her sister. I was proud as a queen when I took them out for a walk, and soon they both adored me. They cried when I wasn't at home and were ecstatic when I returned. My taste for life came back again.

I started to smile and people began to notice me. I was invited out and made some good friends. Without realising it, I was emerging from a long period of grief that had lasted for eight years. It had taken being needed for me to find my place in the world.

I felt I had a purpose again.

The children were crying their eyes out as we loaded the last box into the car, and I wasn't far off myself. But I was 21 years old now and it was high time I became more independent. I wasn't going far. My boyfriend and I had found a small, one-bed flat. It was only a few tram stops away from my sister's house and would be my new home.

I went back to my sister's place to see the children whenever I had the chance. I supervised their homework when their mother came home late from work. Above all, I talked to them. I tried to give them what I hadn't had, what I hadn't known how to ask for: a listening ear. Alice had a demanding job; she was very successful, but her schedule was punishing. With four children to look after, she was exhausted. My uncle also worked a lot. Both were too busy to pay full attention to the heartaches, playground squabbles and daydreams of the two little ones. But I had all the time in the world for them. I was never so happy as when sitting on the floor in their room, listening to their chatter.

I found my first job. I wanted to follow in my mother's footsteps and devote myself to caring for others, so I trained as a special needs support worker. At first, I gained experience working with teenagers. After this, my first full-time post was working with people with disabilities in a residential centre at Kremlin-Bicêtre. I'm ashamed to admit that I wasn't keen at the prospect. I imagined myself in a room full of funny looking people with saliva dribbling from their lips, slumped in a squalid institution. But I'd only just qualified and was hardly being overwhelmed by job offers, so I accepted.

On the first day I went to the centre with my stomach in knots. But I'd resolved to put on a brave front and steeled myself. I did find myself facing some adults with strange looking faces and others with saliva hanging from their mouths. Yet among them, I would experience humanity in all its richness.

From the first moment, the importance of the support workers' role was clear. The adults who had ended up in the centre suffered from various handicaps, but all responded with gratitude and humour to any show of affection, or simply of respect. Working with them changed my understanding of disability. I became more mature, trying to help people who sometimes reacted unpredictably. I learned how to really listen. I developed my capacity to empathise and I realised that it was like a muscle, which became stronger the more it was exercised. I no longer needed to steel myself as I had the first day when faced by the suffering and the distress of the people I was caring for. Instead, I opened myself up and listened to them.

I felt greatly rewarded for my efforts. The slightest bit of attention I gave, the smallest kindness, was given back to me one hundredfold, with total spontaneity and an absolute lack of any agenda. The days were long and sometimes hard. There were crises; of anxiety, of epilepsy, of fever. My job was all encompassing, testing to the full my psychological and physical strength, and my patience. Sometimes I cried from exhaustion when I came back home. But each time I toyed with the idea of stopping, something pulled me back: a look, a smile, an outstretched hand.

What's more, it was through this work that I found my mother.

By taking care of others, by making myself useful, I discovered what had driven her when she was alive. Sometimes memories that had disappeared would come back to me unexpectedly during the juddering metro ride home. I was able to tell myself she'd have been proud of me. I didn't talk about this to anyone, not to my sister or my aunts, but I cherished the memory of her deep in my heart. My life still revolved around her and I knew it was better to keep this to myself; no one would understand that, so long after her death, I was still wrapped up in my long gone mother.

Then, through mutual friends, I met Julien and fell in love with him – with his serenity, his maturity and his self-belief. I had total confidence in him from the start. It felt as though we'd known each other forever; it was just so natural between us. We were both coming out of long-term relationships and were looking for something serious, right from the start. Julien was older than me and already had two daughters, but I wanted to start a family and we talked early on about having a child. For the first time in my life perhaps, it seemed that I, too, could be happy.

When I learned I was pregnant, I knew that I had to change my job. It would be impossible to continue – the long commute was wearing me out and having to help patients out of their wheelchairs or up from the floor after a fall could be risky for my pregnancy. But I cried fat tears when my last day was over, and I said goodbye to the patients and colleagues with whom I'd shared such intense moments.

Hugo was a year old. Soon he'd be going to nursery school. He was a lively little boy, fit and healthy, who was already eyeing the other toddlers in the park with curiosity. Even though I felt he was ready, I hesitated a bit. He'd have to leave the little bubble I'd built around us, where it was just us two every day until Julien, who was a teacher, came home in the evening.

I'd have to leave this enchanted bubble too, to return to the world outside where I'd once again be confronted with everyday life. Was I afraid? Was the bad old shadow of depression that had followed me for so long looming over me again? I didn't want to think about it and chased away the black thoughts. I wanted to be a strong and reassuring mother for my son and I refused to allow myself to be engulfed by it.

I looked for work close to home. Hugo was my priority and I didn't want to be getting back too late in the evenings. I soon found my dream job at a community centre in the neighbouring town, where I'd be in charge of helping local families.

Situated several kilometres to the south of Versailles, the town was wealthy and largely middle-class. Several large businesses had their headquarters there. Yet it bordered some impoverished housing estates and within these neighbourhoods, you would see people who were obviously struggling. It was here that the community centre was situated.

The first few days at the crèche went well for Hugo, who had a whale of a time with the other children. I dropped him off there in the morning on my way to work. My sister worked irregular hours, sometimes coming home in the early afternoon and picking him up. Otherwise, Julien would collect him on the way back from school. As for me, my shifts varied day by day, but we managed somehow. Our little system worked well and everything was chugging along smoothly.

Yet I had the feeling that there was something missing. A feeling of dissatisfaction, of a lack of accomplishment that never left me completely at peace. I had become a mother. I worked. I was married. Life went on. But something wasn't right. I couldn't believe that this was it. There *had* to be something more to life – surely? Sometimes I'd look around me – on the bus, in the supermarket, on the street – at the faces passing by. All those secrets, those lives of which I knew nothing. Were they happy? Was this world was enough for them? It seemed precious little to me. The bleakness that had spread through my childhood was back, like an old companion that hung around me through night and day. I adapted to it. I learned to take advantage of the highs and to wait for the lows to pass. They always passed in the end. So I just waited.

I lost my taste for life. Our evenings became sad. We'd been such a close and happy couple, but now I felt as if we had nothing to share any more. As soon as Hugo was in bed, silence fell on the house. I feared we had nothing in common aside from our son. Julien watched me withdrawing and I could see he didn't understand. "Isn't it enough for you, Sophie?" I imagined him thinking. "The joy, a peaceful life, the calm, the peace – isn't it enough for you?"

No. It wasn't enough.

I couldn't find the words for what was haunting me. I just couldn't believe that my only mission on earth was to be the best mother possible and to live, one day after another, until my death. That couldn't be all. It was impossible.

The days at the community centre were filled with the colour that my nights at home had lost. I liked my colleagues and put my heart and soul into the job, which mainly involved supporting families of North and West African origin. I listened to them, advised them and was there for them when they had problems. These could be in health, schooling, work, children – or anything else. I became an expert in greasing administrative wheels, in knowing which doors to knock on and how to make things move faster.

It was usually the mothers who came first. Intimidated yet determined at the same time, they could be pushy, saying exactly what they thought. They had humour, and were motivated by the desire for change. Their foreheads were creased with worries, yet they'd still burst into great gusts of laughter. They juggled with the difficulties of daily life. They worked, they raised children, they endured sleepless nights worrying about the future and supervised homework they didn't always understand themselves. "Pull yourself together and off you go," they'd gruffly tell their crying child on the first day back at school and walk away without looking behind them, hiding their own tears as they wiped them away. They applied plasters to grazed knees. They were cunning, scheming, generous, warm and ready to do anything for their families. Hospitable, elegant, full of humour and courage – I felt as though I was falling in love with these women because in each of them I found something of my own mother. All of them possessed the same kind of radiant energy, the memory of which inspired and pained me at the same time.

Behind them would be a cheerful, boisterous band of children who'd tumble into the homework club and the games library every evening after school. Then there were the older ones – the cliques of sharp-talking, wary-eyed teenage girls, their hair drawn back tightly into pony tails, their clothes artfully dishevelled. They were inseparable; you never saw one without all the others. Expert at sucking their teeth and other onomatopoeic insults, they'd spend the

afternoons mercilessly dissecting the relationships of everyone they knew. Nothing escaped them.

And then there were the boys. They'd swagger into the
place, aloof and defiant, thronging in the stairwells like a
flock of birds. Full of bluster, they'd rather let themselves be
cut up in slices than show any weakness. Yet they were oblig-
ing, kind and respectful of their elders. It only took a simple
"hello" to prompt a chorus of greetings. "Hello Miss!",
"Don't call her 'Miss', it's Sophie. How are you? Can I help
you carry your bag?" "Don't suck up, yo!" They were funny;
tough, chippy jokers, as merciless as their sisters.

Our ambition – that of all the support workers there – was
to find and encourage common ground between different
communities. We tried to mix everyone together; different
generations, ethnic groups and genders. We organised afternoon tea, evening events and performances. The women
would turn up in groups, wearing colourful outfits. Armed
with tupperware boxes and plates wrapped with aluminium
foil, they'd place the mountains of food on tables covered
with paper tablecloths. Senegalese fish and rice, fermented
cassava, *jollof* rice, peanut sauce, okra, Senegalese chicken,
cakes made from dates and honey, sweet and savoury
doughnuts, Algerian *halwa, shakshuka*...Then they'd sit in
groups and talk and laugh while their sons moved around
the hall like a pack of wolves, constantly looking around
themselves. Then they'd lean against the wall, jostling with
each other and swapping insults, always slightly on edge.
They were cowed by the presence of the mothers, but most
of all by the teenage girls who sat on each other's laps, making barbed remarks about everyone who passed in front of
their sharp eyes.

As for us organisers, we'd circulate all evening from one
group to another. Things didn't necessarily work out as
planned, but there was always a good atmosphere.

We also arranged cultural afternoons, mainly attended by
the women. There too, we met with some problems. The
French women, or at least those who considered themselves

as such – that is to say, those who didn't come from immi-grant communities – complained when the others spoke in Arabic. I did explain the importance of speaking French during these outings, and at the centre in general, to the mothers who came from the north African families.

"It's not nice to be with you if you're all speaking Arabic. It doesn't seem that you want to mix with the others. They might feel excluded."

"I'm not sure they want to mix with us either," retorted one women I liked a lot.

"Well, I don't speak Arabic and I'd like to understand what you're talking about too."

"You're different!"

They promised to make an effort, but as soon as they were all together, they forgot and started speaking Arabic again. It was force of habit. We didn't give up though.

One of the women who regularly attended our cultural afternoons, came to see me in my office one day.

"I really like coming to the outings you organise, Sophie, but there are too many women like....like her."

She motioned with her chin towards an African woman passing by in the corridor, on her way to pick up her son from the homework club. I stiffened.

"What do you mean?"

"You know what I mean. They aren't really interested in culture. They just come to mix with each other. It would be good if you could organise groups which were a bit more... I mean a bit less..."

"Have you looked at me, Christiane?' I asked her in a rather dry voice.

"Oh, but you're different," she said, avoiding the question.

That, at least, was something everyone could agree on.

All these initiatives generally ended in failure, of course. Our good intentions ran into prejudice, ingrained habits and the problem of people wanting to stay with their own kind, whether this was voluntary or imposed. We battled against bad practices, apathy in some quarters and a lack of faith in what we were trying to achieve. But we didn't give up the fight. We had evening team meetings, where the heads of the different services would come together to brainstorm new ideas and potential solutions. We were despondent in turns – when one of us felt ready to throw in the towel, someone else would be there to motivate them and we'd start again. Cooking competitions gave way to Zumba classes, singing evenings to day trips. We started afresh, over and over again, each time with renewed enthusiasm. Our work was essential – it was a question of helping French people from all over the world mix together, to make them aware they formed one community. Utopian perhaps, but we tried.

When I came home in the evenings, I only had any energy for Hugo. Then I'd collapse. Julien and I had grown apart from each other, without any screaming and shouting, anger or hatred. It happened almost without us realising it.

My family still went regularly to the Christian churches in Seine-Saint-Denis and Yvelines, but I hadn't been observant since my mother's death. The rituals, songs and happy atmosphere of the congregation all seemed forced to me. I couldn't identify with the hymns they sang in full voice, or in the way they danced. I'd left the religion of my mother in Yaoundé, and since then there had been an empty space.

It was Islam that would fill it.

I didn't meet a persuasive imam or visionary preacher. No firebrand crossed my path, no one sought me out to show me the way or brainwash me. The religion wasn't handed down or imposed on me. I chose it alone. My journey contradicts the notion that proselytising imams are at work to recruit the good people of France. I met my first imam after I'd already decided to become a Muslim, and I'm not the only one.

Islam wasn't the only religion at the community centre but it was the most commonplace, both among the families we were supporting and the staff. The practices seemed to vary as much as the individuals who followed it. You heard people talk about the more commonly observed festivals and rituals, like Ramadhan and Eid ul-Adha, but everyone went about it their own way.

Some women covered their hair, but not all. Even among those who did, there were significant variations between the simple headscarf and the hijab. Aside from the prohibition on eating pork, which was unanimously respected, practices seemed supple. I often talked about religion with Aïcha, a mother from one of the families I was working with. Far from being sanctimonious or fanatical, she'd thought a lot about her religion and our discussions did me good. I did some research on the internet and bought some books: a Qur'an, of course, as well as a large collection of *hadiths*,[1] grouped under the title *Sahih al-Bukhari*. These related to the life and relationships of the prophet, and were collated by the Persian scholar Mohammed Al-Bukhari in the 9th century. I also had a children's book to learn how to pray. As I studied, I discovered certain things that touched me to the core.

To start with, the fact that there's no need for an intermediary between Allah and the believer seemed a good thing to me. I approved of the obligation to give to charity and to work on oneself. Islam advocates tolerance, even if this is not how it appears today. Its rules can be adapted to each particular situation – if someone is sick, or a woman has her period, they are excused from fasting during Ramadhan. It's the responsibility of the individual to judge whether they have the strength and stamina to do it. As I understood it, the religion was far from being hypocritical in its aims. Appearances weren't important; it was what was on the inside that mattered.

And so it was that I became my own pathway to Islam. I taught myself. I became a Muslim in secret at first. It was a profound, intimate journey and I spoke little about it.

---

1   The hadith are reports of statements or actions of Muhammad, or of his tacit approval or criticism of something said or done in his presence.

The religion would fill the emptiness in in my heart more or less completely. I started to think that the key to a meaningful existence rested in religion, and more specifically in the practice of Islam. It was a personal journey. Stopping eating pork wasn't easy, because I didn't understand why. It didn't correspond to anything that seemed important to me, but I obeyed the rule. On the other hand, the daily practice of acts of charity, of training one's heart to be open to the suffering of others, clearly made sense. When we shield ourselves, we avoid seeing all the forgotten people in our system, erasing them from our field of vision. We chase them from our thoughts, because if we let them enter they would spoil our happiness. Would we be able to eat, laugh and sleep in peace if we were always thinking about the sadness and distress experienced by other people, the same as us? So we close our eyes. Islam does not allow this selfish response and proposes a practical solution, because it is a pragmatic religion.

I converted one winter afternoon and the total absence of ceremony confirmed my desire to continue on this intimate, personal road. It took place in a local mosque. The *shahada*, the profession of faith, only needs two (male) Muslim witnesses. It can take place anywhere. It includes the declaration that the person has made the decision of their own free will, and then one joins the community of believers.

I had been to see an imam at the end of women's prayers one Friday. In a few words, I told about my life and my wish to convert. He listened to me kindly, then advised me to go on learning about the religion. As soon as I felt I was ready, I went back to see him and he found me two witnesses. On the appointed day, my friend Aïcha and her two children came with me. We gathered in a room, plainly furnished with sofas pushed against three of the walls, covered with cushions. There were some framed *surats*[2] written in Arabic that I didn't yet know how to read, as I'd only just started

---

2   Verses from the Qur'an.

learning classical Arabic. A window opened onto the space between the buildings. It was impeccably clean.

The ceremony was very simple. In front of my witnesses and my friend, I pronounced the words that I had learnt by heart: *"Ahadou an la ilaha illallahou wa ahadou anna mou-hammadan rasouloullah,"* which means, "I confirm my belief that there is no god except Allah and Mohammed was his messenger."

And that was that. I was a Muslim.

We drank a cup of tea and talked. I was happy, but not over-excited. From now on, I thought to myself, perhaps my prayers and wishes would be heard. We left in the rain.

I hadn't said anything to Julien. Born into a provincial Catholic family, my husband was a fervent atheist. He always said he'd been traumatised by the Catechism and considered all religions to be mind-numbing. As far as he was concerned, they were either at the root of the worst massacres the human race had gone through, or had supported them. The three monotheistic religions were all the same to him. The church was a cult, faith was voluntary indoctrination – or madness – and religious practices were programmed in, then followed blindly. I'd never make him understand what converting meant to me and had no desire to be laughed at. Better to keep it to myself.

I went on cooking the same food at home, but he remarked upon the fact that I no longer ate pork. He couldn't fail to notice, of course, that I started covering my head after a few months. I didn't want to cover all traces of my hair; it wasn't a question of wearing a hijab. I wasn't the daughter of a woman as independent as my mother for nothing; I was a feminist. A light cloth on the hair and across the chest was enough to conform to the Islamic injunction on modesty. According to the religion, men were also supposed to keep parts of their bodies covered. I was still stylish and took care with my appearance, but I began wearing a turban knotted around my head. Julian watched from the corner of his eye, distrustful but silent.

On Saturday, he was at the market with Hugo while I was at community centre organising a theme night, when he bumped into Aïcha.

"So you didn't mind that Sophie converted?" she asked him.

He was shocked, but avoided the question and replied with some banal comment. But when I came home later that evening, he was incredulous.

"You converted to Islam and didn't talk to me about it?"

"I knew that you wouldn't be interested. I didn't want to upset you."

Julien looked dejected.

"I would've listened if you'd talked to me about it."

"I know religion isn't your thing. But it makes me feel good. That's all."

"As long as you don't become a crazy fundo. You know the new converts are always the worst..."

"No risk of that."

I held up my hand, categorically signifying the end of the discussion.

That was all. We never spoke about more than that. But of course, not sharing this momentous event with him, something so important to me, contributed to the distance growing between us. There wasn't much left of a relationship left, now we'd stopped confiding in one another. I brought a small prayer rug home that I kept rolled up in a corner, and I made sure that my faith didn't take over the house. Julien and I agreed on one thing at least, that religion is a private matter.

At the community centre, word soon spread even though I was discreet. Some people congratulated me, although it wasn't at the centre of our discussions. Conversions have always taken place where there are different religions present, and this was also a subject of satisfaction. People don't always remain attached to the beliefs they started out with. You can come across a religion and choose it for yourself. It's a personal journey, or at least it should be.

Yet my conversion didn't bring me peace. It was just one step in a very long, profound moral crisis. Islam did not provide a solution, but it did give me the tools for reflection – other avenues for thinking about the world. I was going through a torturous process, trying to work out my meaning in life. When I spoke to Julien about it again, he just asked why I needed a meaning.

"Make the most of what you have, savour it and share with others. It's enough for everyone else, why not you?"

Why what was enough for him wasn't enough for me was the crux of the question and I was incapable of answering it. There had to be a meaning to everything. I needed there to be one. To use a religious image, I was searching like a creature in the dark. This was truly how I felt, like a blind insect, flying into the same window over and over again, while all I needed was a helping hand to open it and let me fly towards the sky. Towards the light.

The management of the community centre changed. The new team was close to the right-wing council, which took a hard line on the issues of immigration, delinquency and security. It was a sign of the times. Some of our grants were cut. The social and cultural programmes were the first targets. A whole section of the community centre's budget was amputated. One after the other, our projects were closed down with only those that were profit making allowed to remain. This drove me crazy as it was in direct conflict with our social mission.

We wanted to organise a memorial exhibition around the theme of the slave trade. The town hall refused vociferously, arguing that the subject was too divisive. But if you refuse to face up to your own history, you become cut off from yourself; things don't cease to exist because you don't talk about them. The motives behind this refusal made me furious. Couldn't they see that *they* were the ones making divisions? They were sowing bad feeling and mistrust in people's hearts.

We drafted requests for financial help, which we sent to the relevant authorities in the town hall. We sent them dossiers as thick as telephone directories informing them of the dozens of questionnaires we'd carried out, with stacks of supporting documents stapled inside. But it was all in vain.

Over the past year I'd been giving a Zumba class twice a week, which had been a great success. The waiting list was as long as my arm. I explained that I'd been doing this voluntarily, during my spare time, because the community centre hadn't been able to release the funds to pay me. The women who came to my class enjoyed it so much that I couldn't bring myself to give it up. I asked for some training, to make sure I didn't make any mistakes which could injure anyone; all I knew was what I'd learned from going to the gym myself and taking dance classes. I conscientiously reproduced what I'd seen, but had no formal training. It was a legal obligation to be qualified in order to give these kinds of classes. I didn't want to practice illegally. I wanted to be professional about it.

They refused my first application. Then they lost my file and I had to start all over again. I lost hours in tedious, administrative tasks. My second request was also turned down. I asked again. After giving the class for free for two years, I felt I very much deserved this training. But the person responsible for training went on extended sick leave, and no one could tell me who was looking after her files.

People from the town hall started to come for visits, which felt more like inspections. They'd arrive in a hurry and would only speak to the management, ignoring the youths who'd immediately put on their act of swaggering bravado when they saw them. Then these town hall representatives would come to our office and give us their verdict.

"A lot of baseball caps out there. You don't tell them to take them off?"

"This isn't a school. We prefer that they feel comfortable here, that they feel confident and that they come at all, rather that grilling them on what they wear."

"And the Arabic? Some of the women complained that there's more Arabic than French spoken at the community centre."

"This is an exaggeration. There's a group of mums who don't have much chance to get out and see each other. They really enjoy getting together and they speak Arabic without thinking. We've talked to them about this and they *do* make an effort to speak French."

"No desire to integrate, basically..."

"This isn't a question of integration, I think. These women are French and have made their lives here. Their children are French and most of them don't even speak Arabic. Imagine if a French family moves to the US and meets another French family there. The two families will enjoy speaking to each other in French. That's all."

The town hall officials didn't seem convinced.

"And the youngsters hanging around there, doing nothing. What activities are they signed up for?"

"Mostly nothing. They just like meeting up here. It's a community centre. We see that as proof of our success, of our acceptance in the community,' my boss replied evenly.

"They didn't even say 'hello'," grumbled one of the councillors.

"You didn't say hello to them either!"

My reply shot out before I could stop myself. The official didn't know how to react. Meetings like this came one after another and were all the same. It was obvious the direction of the wind was changing.

4: The Boys

I called them "the boys." Idriss, Mohammed and Souleymane had been friends since childhood, the three of them growing up together in a working-class neighbourhood. Idriss and Mohammed were from the same block of flats, while Souleymane lived in a small house next door. Their families knew each other and they'd been inseparable since nursery school. They'd been through kindergarten together, then primary school and secondary school. They'd all chosen the same line of work, as electricians. Mohammed had been the most successful. He had a permanent position and earned well. Idriss and Souleymane worked here and there, taking whatever they could find. Their income was less regular and they were often paid in cash, but they had enough money to get by and to help their families. They were good kids.

At the time.

Idriss's family was originally from Senegal, although he'd never been there and all five children in the family were born in France. His father worked and his mother was a housewife. She was a warm natured, plump woman with a glowing smile. Mohammed's family had come to France nearly 50 years ago, from Morocco. He'd never been there either. Both his parents worked; his father on construction sites and his mother in a school canteen. They weren't practising Muslims and his mother never wore a headscarf, although they did celebrate Ramadhan. Souleymane came from Burkina Faso. I knew his family the least well of the three. Coming from a polygamous household, he had numerous brothers and sisters.

Idriss' mother was very maternal. The first time I met her, she gave me a big hug. She often came and dropped off a Tupperware box of whatever she'd cooked that day to thank me for writing a recommendation letter for one of her children, who'd wanted to run some activities at a local school. I became closer to the family when one of Idriss's aunts came to France for medical care during a difficult pregnancy. After the birth, the baby stayed in hospital and I tried to help as much as possible with the arrangements and communication with the hospital, as well as giving moral support. I spent my days going back and forth between mother and child. I was so involved that Julien pulled me up on it. He felt that the families were taking advantage of me and that I'd be better off spending more time with Hugo. But I felt the need to devote myself to something outside the narrow confines of my own home.

I quickly felt adopted by Idriss' family, even though our relationship mainly revolved around the community centre and the events I organised. The younger brothers and sisters were enrolled in the homework club. I supported the mothers in negotiating the labyrinthine administrative system. They'd regularly bring me thick files, which we'd try to make sense of together. I'd help them to draft responses and did my best to understand what they were going through.

One of Idriss's sisters had signed up for the Zumba class, which didn't please her brother. He said that Zumba was "erotic dancing." He was laughing when he said it, in front of a room full of people. Who would have thought that he really meant it? Of the three friends he was the most charismatic – and the toughest. But he loved his mother, never grumbling if he was asked to help out, and he had a good sense of humour.

Mohammed's mother had come on a visit to the Louvre we'd organised one time. Paris was only 25 kilometres away, but she'd hardly ever been there. We went to see the display of Egyptian antiquities on a Sunday when it was free, ending up next to one of the mummies. She was so impressed.

"Goodness, what beautiful things there are here!" she exclaimed, gesturing theatrically with her hands, over and over again.

In the train on the way back, she hugged me like a long lost sister. She never came on any other visits, despite my efforts. It was hard for her to take time out from her family commitments, even for just one afternoon. I missed her cheerfulness and enthusiasm, at once childlike and sincere. She made no pretence of being sophisticated, she was just genuine and honest.

And then, one day, the boys were gone.

It was one of Idriss's sisters who told me. I was in my office on my lunchbreak when the phone rang. It was September 2014.

"Sophie, they've gone!" Mum's in hysterics. Ibra, Momo and Souleymane...they've gone to Syria!"

"I'm coming!" I gasped.

Abdulaye, Idriss's younger brother, had received a message from him saying he'd left France for good. Abdulaye told the family and everyone gathered together in the cramped apartment, trying to make sense of what had happened. The three young men, along with a friend who had a car, had gone to Spain four days earlier on the pretence they were taking a holiday. When they arrived at their destination, they told the driver what their real plan was: to catch a flight to Turkey and head to Syria. Their friend, in tears, did everything he could to persuade them not to go, but in vain. He came back alone, not daring to say anything to anyone. He was terrified of being accused of helping them.

Idriss's mother shook with sobs.

"He didn't even say goodbye! Not even a hug!"

She went back over last few days before they'd left. She thought she remembered that Idriss had looked sad. I listened to her, incredulous, understanding that her universe had just shrunk and that from now on, her life would be divided into before and after her son left.

It wasn't the first time I'd heard about this happening, but this was the first young man I knew personally who'd gone. It was said that around 60 people from neighbouring towns had left during the past few years. We talked about it sometimes with the young people at the community centre – it was part of daily life for all of us, more or less. All of them knew someone who'd gone. It was a subject of fantasy, of fear or of bragging – and of endless discussions. But until that day, it had never been reality for me.

Everyone was crying in the small, packed living room. Idriss's father had rushed back from work and was sitting down, looking helpless and stunned. Some neighbours and friends had come over to offer their support, and the conversation went round and round. "How did you find out? When did they go? Were there any signs before they left? What a tragedy!"

Suddenly the landline telephone rang.

Idriss's mother was the fastest, diving onto the handset. It was Idriss.

Always close to his mother, he wanted to reassure her he was OK. But she wouldn't let him get a word in.

"Come back, come back! It's not too late. It's just a stupid mistake, no one knows about it. You have to come back now!" she cried into the phone.

She continued to repeat the same thing, helplessly. She didn't know that the three of them were already in Syria. They were in Raqqa, the "capital" of the Islamic State and returning was no longer an option.

When she hung up, her sobbing grew harder. Her husband remained silent and stupefied. Tears welled up inside me at seeing them so devastated and I watched, powerless, as the women wept.

During the following days and weeks, we spoke of nothing else. I went every day to see the families to get updates. I'd sit in the living room, listening to them asking themselves the same question over and over again. What could have happened to make three good kids, with no history of this kind of thing, do something like this? We learned that the three boys had taken out loans before they left.

I learned that they kept up almost daily contact with their mothers, their brothers, their sisters and some of their friends. They showed me some of their messages.

"Hi, how's it going? And how's mum? Life is beautiful here. Tell mum I'm sending her a big hug. And smash the athletics! May Allah watch over you."

This was sent to Majid, Mohammed's younger brother. The message had a photo of Mohammed attached to it, doing a back flip above a river. In the lower right hand corner of the picture you could see a hand making a two fingered victory salute.

Majid, the younger brother, was on cloud nine. He glowed with pride. The mobile was passed from hand to hand in the living room, in a silence loaded with sombre thoughts; the relief of knowing the boys were alive competing with anger at the contrast between the happy, carefree photo, and the desolation they'd left behind. Mohammed's mother kept swiping the screen to look, once more, at her son smiling and having fun. She could not believe her eyes.

Where were they? They hadn't said a word about that. Behind the gymnastic Mohammed, you could see a vast plain of bronze earth. The river was a brilliant blue-green. No clues there. No village, no buildings in the background. Just this young man, playing like a child. All the same, you could sense some guilt behind the words, "And how's mum?"

From that day onwards, the boys communicated with their families all the time, the messing coming regularly on Viber or Messenger. They gave news of their health (which was good), and reassured their parents through their brothers and sisters (life was wonderful; they were sharing a beautiful, large apartment; they were being payed). Nothing specific, no names, no locations. It was clear they were in Syria, but they were secretive. They also asked to be kept up to date about what was going on in France – what was happening at school, how their brothers had done in sports events, and the usual little details of family life. They wouldn't respond to direct questions, but their messages had a comforting air.

I wondered if they missed us and if they regretted going. I watched their mothers fall apart and asked myself how they could have just left like that. Because they loved their mothers, loved them as you love someone you've seen working their fingers to the bone for you. They loved them painfully, fully aware of all the humiliation and the sacrifices they'd gone through for their families. They loved their mothers as good sons do, and they knew full well that they'd broken their hearts.

One day, Idriss's sister showed me a photo of him grimacing at the camera. The look on his face worried me; it was the look of a fanatic, and it reminded me of Shekau, the head of Boko Haram. It scared me. I wondered if he was on drugs.

We talked about it a lot at the community centre. For us, it was the sudden entrance – very real, very brutal – of international politics and religion into our everyday lives. We discussed it amongst ourselves, going over and over the behaviour of the three in the months before they left. We knew them well. Some of us, who'd been there for a long time, had known them throughout their schooldays. What had happened? Did we miss something that could have warned us? Had there been any signs? But the boys had been no different from the others. Like other boys their age from the housing estates, they were pro-Palestinian rather than pro-Israeli. They thought the media was untrustworthy, and that the government disseminated propaganda. They felt that Muslims were looked down on in France, and that the US had lied about Iraq. They believed the conspiracy theories that spread like wildfire on the internet – this was their only intellectual arsenal. They didn't read newspapers and hardly watched the television.

They weren't wrong on all counts, at least as far as I was concerned. But fundamentally they were no different from other boys their age; the only thing that stood out was the strong friendship between them, which explained why they left together and not alone.

We didn't pick up on any "signs of radicalisation," like you read about in the newspapers. I hadn't noticed any change in their behaviour. All three of them had started thinking more their religion in their teens. They prayed. And it's true that the three young men I called "the boys" were more interested in hanging around with each other than with girls. They preferred to shake my hand than kiss me on the cheek – but they weren't the only ones. They went regularly to a neighbourhood mosque. Nothing more. No aggressive arguments. No propaganda. No political flights of fancy. They didn't grow beards or wear *djellabas*,[3] but dressed in the same tracksuit bottoms, jeans and jackets as their friends. We often spoke about religion together, at least since I converted, but I was sure they weren't fanatics. We'd discuss certain verses from the Qur'an, sometimes in the way of a debate, sometimes even jokingly. They never talked as if they were in possession of some superior truth.

I remember one day Idriss saying boastfully to myself and one of the other female employees, that he'd never buy a dishwasher for his wife, that she'd have to wash the plates herself. He was obviously trying to wind us up and we told him, "When you grow up Idriss, you'll find out who's really in charge of the household!" Idriss was 23 years old, but he'd never been in a serious relationship with a girl.

"I bet that one day, when you're married, I'll come to your house one evening and it'll be you I'll find washing the dishes," I teased him. We'd laughed for a moment. Even today, I can hardly believe that he was serious.

Other things came back to me, though. Idriss – it was always him, because he was the most assertive one – had often said he was against dancing. Usually I'd tell him off,

---

3   A long, loose-fitting unisex outer robe with full sleeves, worn in the
    Maghreb region of North Africa and in Arabic-speaking countries
    along the Mediterranean.

and he'd back down saying he was only joking. Now I wondered.

Once the families told the police they'd gone, there'd no longer be any chance of the boys coming back under the radar. The DGSI[4] would open files on them, and if they came back – which was what everyone was praying for – they'd be interrogated, then sent to prison for several months at the very least. Their mothers were worried about this. *At the same time*, they thought, *they're also French and if we tell the police they've left, there's a chance, perhaps, that the government will try to get them back.*

Someone must have persuaded them to go, they told themselves. It just wasn't possible that good boys like theirs could have thought of it alone. They had everything here in France. Work, loving families, and the rest of their lives in front of them. What had come over them to throw it all away and run off to a foreign country, a country at war? Their parents couldn't understand at all and were in despair. Yet I saw several of their younger brothers, despite their tears, showing a certain pride in what they considered to be the courage of their siblings. It was their age, of course.

"But why?" Julien was indignant when I told him what had happened. "They wanted an adventure? They were bored here? Is it their Spanish Civil War or something? Isn't there another cause they could have chosen?"

"Which cause?"

"Good God, there are plenty of causes! I don't know – orphans in Guatemala, refugees..."

"But who are you to judge the good causes from the bad ones?"

I didn't know why I was arguing about it. I didn't believe entirely in what I was saying myself. But I felt the need, I don't know why, to defend the choice of "the boys" to Julien.

"The boys? You talk about them as if they were children."

---

4   The Director General for Internal Security; the French equivalent of MI5.

"They are children."

Julien didn't reply.

In the end, the families had to face reality. It was neither a mistake, nor had they gone on a whim. Their sons' Facebook accounts were no longer active, nor were their mobile phones. The boys weren't coming back. Each couple, their hearts breaking, took themselves to the police station to inform them about the departure of their beloved children for jihad. I couldn't imagine greater pain for a parent than this. The police came and searched their apartments, confiscating their computers. They found nothing conclusive. The boys had covered their tracks.

The long period of waiting began. The families kept praying that one beautiful morning their wayward children would reappear, confused and contrite. What a telling off they'd give them! The mothers would luxuriate in this fantasy, while the fathers would remain in pessimistic silence, Meanwhile, the boys' younger brothers went on boasting to their friends about the messages on their mobile phones from Syria. *Yeah, man.*

The atmosphere was of a family in mourning. I recognised it. I watched Mohammed's mother disintegrate, no longer sleeping or eating. I visited as often as possible on the way back from work. Sometimes I brought some food I'd cooked the night before. I'd sit down next to her on the sofa and listen as the memories of her son's childhood spilled out. How well behaved he'd been in nursery school, how the teacher had said he was a promising student. The time when he'd come home crying because one of the other kids had hit him in the playground. He hadn't always been comfortable with the other children; in gym class he'd never been able to climb up to the top of the rope, which had given him a terrible complex. Idriss, though, was a lot more sporty and had always helped him. She hoped no one would harm him and that he wouldn't harm anyone either. She hoped that they would stay together, the three friends protecting each other. Idriss and Souleymane would watch over Mohammed.

But she couldn't believe they'd done such a thing. Taking up weapons? Joining an army? Going to war? It was unimaginable. He, who had always carried the shopping bags? He, who had protected the younger ones? He, who was so kind?

And she'd start to cry inconsolably again. What had she missed? What could they have done to make their children leave?

5: Recruited

One evening in December, as I was getting ready for bed, I heard Skype ringing on my mobile. It was a hidden number. I answered.

"Guess who it is!" said a male voice.

I had no idea, and I wasn't in a good mood. I'd had my tonsils removed that day, and I didn't feel like messing around.

"I have no idea, and unless you tell me who you are, I'm going to hang up."

"Sophie, it's me – it's Idriss!"

And that's how it started.

In the beginning, Idriss simply wanted news from home. He thanked me for helping out with their families. I didn't hide that fact from him that his mother was getting worse. His seven-year-old sister was asking questions non-stop, too. Our first discussion was good; I was hearing the old Idriss, with the same sense of humour, and it was easy to talk to him. I even said to myself that, if I handled this well, I might be able to convince them to come back. I'd have to handle it carefully, but perhaps I could succeed where their families – who were too emotionally involved – had failed. We started speaking regularly.

"I know it's hard," he said to me. "I know it's terrible for mum. Believe me, I can't bear hurting her. But my life is here now. You have to make choices in life. I know I haven't made a mistake."

I soon understood that he wasn't going to come back quietly. I began to see what I'd initially thought as selfishness in a new light. Idriss had made a life choice, which he'd thought about long and hard, and he wasn't about to let anyone change his mind with emotional blackmail. In the beginning, I spoke to him like an older sister during our exchanges, a bit superior, the same tone I'd always used with him. They were kids; although they weren't young enough to have been my children, they could have been younger brothers or nephews. They'd never impressed me and I'd always kept them in their place, albeit with affection. But now, without me realising it, there was a subtle change. Idriss was living through things I had no experience of, which had made him grow up. He was self-assured, without being aggressive. He listened to me as he always had done. He accepted the misery that he'd inflicted on his family, not attempting to shy away from it. But for him, this was a hardship he had to endure as he was in the service of a higher cause, and there were sacrifices he knew he had to make.

We never mentioned the cause itself.

Souleymane and Mohammed started to write to me too. Bit by bit, I became the messenger between them and their families. According to the boys' wishes, I tried to reassure their parents by giving them positive news. I didn't realise I had become part of a well-established propaganda system.

"Imagine how hard it was for us to hide our decision to go," Idriss said to me. "the last weeks were hell. A lot of people don't go through with it at that point. But we held out."

Then Mohammed's mother made a suicide attempt.

It was her daughter Ouafia who found her, unconscious, in the bathroom. She'd taken all the sleeping pills prescribed by the doctor we practically had to force her to visit after her son left. Ouafia had called the emergency services, who turned up very quickly. Her stomach was pumped on the spot, then she was taken to hospital where she recovered.

For this mother of seven children to want to take her own life, she must have felt there was truly no hope left. As soon as I knew that she was going to survive, I sent a brief message to Mohammed. Then I waited. If this news didn't bring him back then nothing would.

My phone was silent for several days. I imagined that he was digesting the news. I started to worry – perhaps something had happened to him?

Then, on the evening of the fourth day, these words popped up on my screen: "May Allah forgive her. Tell her I love her."

They were never coming back.

Our conversations started up again. I'm usually quite discreet and am not in the habit of telling people about my life. Since my childhood, I'd taken care of my problems on my own. So what had changed now? Without doubt, the distance was part of it. If Idriss had been in front of me in his jeans and baseball cap, I'd never have allowed myself to confide in him so much.

But now there was just the screen and his kind replies, always full of his ghetto humour, a bit teasing, a bit immature, which made me smile. Sometimes he'd cite a *surat* which would speak to me, making me reflect on my point of view or opening up a new perspective. I wasn't becoming a zealot. But Islam is a religion which doesn't shy away from examining the trivial problems of everyday life, and it helped me see things more clearly.

I hadn't realised how alone I felt. Keeping my conversion practically secret had widened the gulf between myself and the other people around me. Julien was far from my thoughts. My colleagues at the community centre, with whom I'd always got on with very well, weren't interested in religion. At the same time, the new officials at the town hall were suspicious and distrustful of it. I had the impression they'd have looked awry at my conversion had I brought it up. As for my family – forget it. They were such fervent Catholics that I'd have caused an earthquake by admitting I'd become a Muslim.

Idriss, Souleymane and Mohammed all knew I'd converted, and that was all it took to make them closer to me than anyone in my circle. But I thought I knew them better than they knew me. I thought I was in control of the situation.

Our conversations became more and more personal. I could talk to them about my problems at work. It was easy and came naturally. They knew the places and they remembered my colleagues. They could easily imagine what we were coming up against. It was that straightforward. It felt good to confide in them.

Little by little, it started to go further than the boundaries of work. I don't know how I started to bring up the more personal subjects, which I'm not usually in the habit of telling anyone. Later – a lot later – I'd be ashamed to remember this. For a long time it would be impossible to admit that I'd trusted these boys. These kids.

But they understood. They knew the feeling of emptiness inside me. The feeling of waste. It was for that reason that they'd left themselves, they told me. I wasn't alone. There was something to be done in this world. A cause to devote yourself to.

A cause whose name we'd still never spoken of.

We started talking about Syria.

"You should see how beautiful this city is, Sophie. It's magical."

"But what about the war? The bombing?"

"That's all bullshit. There's no bombing in Raqqa – the situation is totally stable. The town is so beautiful. We have a big apartment, 120 m2, with two living rooms. You should see it, Sophie, you wouldn't believe your eyes. The streets are full of trees and flowers."

"I'll never see it because I'd never go of my free will to a country at war."

"The war is far away. You don't even hear bombing here – we haven't heard any gunfire since we arrived. Nothing. You shouldn't believe what you read in the newspapers. Here, Muslims from all over the world live in peace. We have a purpose. We're useful."

They started talking about a hospital, for women.

"A lot of families have fled, due to the violence of Bashar, the Syrian president. So there's a lack of staff in the hospitals. For example, the big women's hospital in Raqqa, which cares for Syrian woman from all over the country. A lot of foreigners come to help out, but there aren't enough of them. In the maternity ward, there are an enormous amount of births and not enough people to help them deliver."

"But I'm not a doctor."

"They don't just need doctors and nurses. There's a lack of motivated women to help the patients and to look after their kids. There are huge needs here."

Images began to form in my mind. Of Syrian children playing in a park to forget, for a moment, the hardships of war. Of me, inside a big hospital, holding the hand of a woman stretched out on a bed.

I shook myself. More and more, I felt like I was sleepwalking. I was confused. The depression was interfering with my perception. I felt as though I was in a bubble, that I'd become detached from the world without anyone noticing. I had a secret that grew more and more precious: every day, I was talking with boys who'd left for a country at war.

"There's so much to do here. The Syrian people are suffering and there's not enough of us. Life is really hard for some of them."

"But the women? I've heard that women are badly treated and stoned!"

"Sophie, that's all propaganda. It happened in Kobane, not here. Do you think we'd stay if there were women being tortured in front of our eyes? Do you think we'd accept that?"

I know they wouldn't. Idriss, the good son, the protective brother, the kind boy, would never support such horrors. They sent me photos of themselves in restaurants or mucking around. They looked like holiday snaps. I didn't know what they did all day. I imagined they were in contact with

the local population. We never spoke about politics and
I never heard them praising Daesh.

I didn't have much idea about the situation on the
ground. As far as I was aware, the Islamic State were fighting
against the tyranny of Bashar el-Assad, not against Syrian
fighters. I was ignorant about the other groups. I didn't
know that IS was full of foreign fighters, and that it was also
fighting against the rebels.

It was Idriss who first spoke to me about the invitation
system. He'd envisaged bringing his father over to convince
him that everything was all right. He wanted him to visit
the city, to show him the luxury in which they were living,
so that he could reassure his mother. The idea entered into
my head.

The process was strange and repetitive. The more I talked
to them, the more I listened to them, and the more I believed
them. I was hearing it from the horses' mouth, after all. Who
else knew that much about it? Who else had a contact on the
ground, in the middle of Raqqa, with whom they could talk
so often? I felt chosen, important, and I took pleasure in
storing the details up in my mind.

But as soon as the conversations ended, my worries and
doubts would return to the surface. Syria was at war – this
was impossible to deny. If bombs weren't falling on Raqqa at
the moment, that didn't mean that the town would escape
them in the future.

The words and images were becoming more and more
closely intertwined. They sent me photos of their apartment,
of the park outside the building where children clambered
on a climbing frame. Other photos of a broad, gleaming
river, which I now know was the Euphrates.

Who was it that first talked about me going there? None
of them, I think. It was never put to me clearly, but somehow
seemed to become a foregone conclusion. "You'll see,
Sophie, you'll see that we weren't lying to you." "You won't
believe your eyes when you see our apartment. It's lush!"

"You'll be really useful at the women's hospital. Believe us, you won't regret it."

It was six months since they'd left, and we'd been talking for three months, every day, when I started to think over the practical details of going.

"Could I come for a month?"

"Of course. We'd have to get you a special visa, as you'd be travelling without a man."

I told myself this would be a chance to learn Arabic. It would be a bit like an internship, or an immersion course. I could help people who were suffering from the bombs of a tyrant.

The idea took shape.

I was at an impasse in life. The community centre was bogged down with difficulties. None of our activities to bring the different communities together had really succeeded, as everyone just stayed in their own groups. No one wanted to mix together. People were complaining and suffering, but it seemed to me that it was less and less possible to help them. The tiniest initiative resulted in an endless bureaucratic process of meetings and paperwork, which sapped my spirit. I saw the files piling up in the offices and the unjustified rejection letters from the council. I no longer had the energy to keep trying. Everything was over-regulated, too difficult and too slow.

At home, my marriage was in a deadlock. I felt at a loss. My nieces had grown up; soon they wouldn't need me any-more, now they were becoming teenagers. Friends and boyfriends would take my place – and good for them.

My sister and I didn't speak much about personal issues, but we were still close – instinctively so. Several years before, I went with her to Cameroon. I was the first time I'd been back to the country since my mother died. It was a tough trip. We went past the family home, which seemed ridicu-lously small. Was that the huge house with its tree-filled courtyard that had lived in my dreams for the past 15 years? I couldn't believe it.

I met up with some family members I didn't know, and some I hadn't seen since I left. The cousins I'd grown up were now loud, voluptuous, imposing women. They welcomed me warmly, but we had nothing in common any more. They seemed so self-assured, so calm and so grown-up. I was, and remained forever, an orphan.

I wanted to pay a visit to my father's family in the north of the country, but one of my father's brothers, who I met in Yaoundé, dissuaded me. Regretfully, I gave up on the idea. I'd often thought that it was in those areas where you could really make yourself useful. And there I was, stuck, living my boring little life outside Paris, fighting to keep my Zumba course running. I could do better than that. Time was going by and I needed to do something. I'd always wanted to travel to challenging places – to push my boundaries and to get out of my comfort zone.

I felt that all I had in the world was Hugo. In my eyes, it was very important that he didn't grow up taking the comforts of his life for granted. I didn't want him to think that the rest of the world was the same as what he'd known. I wanted to make my son a man of the world, aware of his luck and willing to share it. I didn't want to bring up a narrow-minded French boy, stuck in his certainties. From the start, before even planning anything, it was clear that whatever I did, Hugo would be with me. There was no question of us being separated.

In January 2015, I went alone to Goree Island in Senegal, to spend a week with Idriss' aunt – the one I'd helped in France during her pregnancy. The trip made a profound impression on me. I was deeply moved when I visited the "House of Slaves"[5]. The "Door of no Return" hit me hard; the opening in the wall looking out onto the sea from which the chained slaves would leave, forever. The image engraved itself on me, feeding my anger and my desire to fight against injustice.

5   The House of Slaves (Maison des Esclaves) and its Door of No Return is a museum and memorial to the Atlantic slave trade.

When I came back from Senegal, I'd reached the tipping point.

Each conversation with the boys came with new explanations and practical details, which made the prospect of going there more and more conceivable. They'd asked for the use of an empty apartment in the same building they lived in. Hugo and I could stay there. They'd contacted the person in charge of the women's hospital, who confirmed they needed all the help they could get. They knew a French woman who'd worked there who didn't speak Arabic either. Even though I didn't have medical training, they'd find a way to make use of me. They had my entry visa and all I had to do was tell them when I wanted to come. They assured me that it would be a powerful experience.

They weren't wrong about that.

I didn't even ask how to get to into Syria. I was relying on them totally by now. They told me to take a flight to Istanbul and to let them know when I arrived. One of their contacts would come and find me.

Like a carnivorous plant that lures an insect into its heart then traps it there, the three of them smoothed out all the bumps in the way. All I had to do was take the first step, in order to glide, hopelessly, towards them. Yet I didn't buy my ticket. Something held me back. I put it off, again and again.

"Sophie, it's France, it's the selfish, modern life which makes us slaves. It's a waste of your energy living like that."

They had a point. I had no more energy. I felt nothing any more. It was only the obligation to show I was an exemplary mother that got me up in the morning to carry out, mechanically, my daily chores: washing, getting ready, waking up Hugo, giving him his breakfast, getting him ready, driving him to nursery school. My son was three years old and there would only be the two of us in the apartment, as Julien left earlier. We'd be alone together in the street, in the bus and on the pavements. Nothing touched me anymore. Everyone around me seemed to be very far away.

For a long time now, I'd learned to recognise this distaste for life, which would periodically overwhelm me. Soon I wouldn't be able to see any solution other than to leave – and by "leave", I mean to die. I would try and hang on to the thought of my nieces and Hugo. I'd destroy their lives irreparably. But it wouldn't make a difference. The desire to die would engulf me. I'd made two attempts in the past.

Since then, I'd learned to spot the warning signs which came before this morbid state of mind, but not to extinguish them. This time, the idea of going to Syria came to me as an escape route from this desire for death. Unless this was the way I'd found to take my life?

I told Julien I wanted to go to Turkey to work as a volunteer in an orphanage. I reckoned on taking Hugo during the February school holidays. Julien had looked after Hugo a lot. He was tired from the week he'd just spent with him while I was in Senegal, and I played on that to convince him. He agreed, but at the same time said that he found my plans confusing. But our marriage had come to a standstill, and he must also have wanted me to take some distance. We decided to take a break from each other and to see how we could change things when I came back.

"I'll have an answer then," I told him. I wasn't lying. I needed to leave, to make myself useful and regain my zest for life.

I bought my ticket for Istanbul, leaving on 20th February. I chose the return date of 10th March, as it was cheaper that way. That wasn't even a month, but the boys said they'd pay for a return trip a bit later. Yet even at that moment, I hesitated. I told myself that I could change my mind at any time. If I no longer felt like going, all I had to do was turn around at the airport. No matter. I'd be left with two unused air tickets, nothing more serious. I'd decide before getting on the plane. This thought helped me remain calm.

Then it was the day of our departure.

Julien drove Hugo and I to the airport. His face was drawn, and he looked sad but we were very gentle with each other. Although we'd grown apart, we'd never stopped loving each other. As for Hugo, he thought we were going on holiday. I'd told my sister that we were going on vacation, too. I was lucky, she'd said to me. Aside from the boys, thousands of miles away, only I knew what the real plan was.

Hugo and I turned back to wave goodbye at his father from the other side of the customs barrier. I turned again a moment later. Julien's long silhouette towered over the tight crowd of travellers. I felt my heart tighten, but kept going.

I was flying into the unknown. After a stopover in Kiev, it wasn't long before we were preparing ready to land in Istanbul. I wondered who would be waiting for us.

In the arrival hall I picked up our luggage and called Idriss.

"Well this is it! We're in Turkey."

"Ok. Wait by the arrival gates, someone will come to find you."

We didn't wait long until a man came to meet us and drove us to the apartment of a Belgian family. With hindsight, I suppose that they were supporters of IS posted behind the lines as part of Daesh's logistic set-up. But we didn't speak much, and I couldn't say so for sure.

The next evening, our host family drove us to the bus station where we boarded a coach to Sanliurfa. The journey lasted all night. I was in touch with Idriss several times, who reassured and encouraged me.

Hugo slept like a log in the bus, and I had to carry him when we got off. He was heavy in my arms and slowed me down a bit. These early days in Turkey were the image of everything that would follow. I was dragging my son off on an adventure and was totally responsible for him. He had no one but me.

In Sanliurfa, a man welcomed us and drove us to a house close to the border. He gave us some food and drink, then showed us to a bedroom but we couldn't communicate. He spoke only Turkish and Arabic, not a word of French or English. I distracted Hugo as best I could.

Finally, the man signalled to me that it was time to go and helped me to carry my suitcases through some fields of olive trees. I didn't notice any barriers, guards or watchtowers, and I didn't know when we'd crossed the frontier. While officially closed, it was extremely porous and trade was still brisk between Turkey and Syria. As I'd soon realise, they wanted for nothing in the Islamic State, with the shops very well stocked. You could find everything there, especially all the popular Turkish brands.

After walking for about ten minutes, we arrived at a tiny hamlet. A 4 x 4 was waiting for us between some farm work-ers' huts. There were two men in the front, dressed impeccably in the Salafist style. They both wore a kind of long cotton shirt reaching to the knees over baggy, Afghan style trousers, scarves around their necks, with long hair and beards. One of them had a sub-machine gun. Hugo and I climbed into the back. The man sat on the passenger seat turned and asked me for our passports. I passed them to him, at the same time vaguely aware I'd just given away something important. I kept the file with my and Hugo's personal documents in my handbag.

The car set off.

I don't know if the two men were friends of the boys, or had simply been sent to pick us up. I didn't ask any ques-tions and they didn't talk to me. We trundled along for several hours. The two men spoke to each other in Arabic, while Hugo and I kept quiet. I looked around me with curi-osity. The landscape was bleak, a vast dusty plain beyond which I could make out some low hills, barely covered with sparse vegetation. Night fell and Hugo slept in my arms. At one point, I noticed the carcass of a military aircraft, a reminder of the war being played out here. But no other trace. No noise of aircraft, no tanks. I don't know what I was expecting, but I was very nervous. I was eager to get to Raqqa and to find the boys. I'd reserve my judgement until then.

From time to time, I cast an eye at the gun which its owner hadn't bothered to conceal. It was the first time I'd see a weapon so close. I hoped they weren't expecting to be attacked by the troops of Bashar al-Assad. I didn't think for a moment that they would use them against the Syrian people.

Hugo, who'd woken up, was calm and attentive, as if he could sense my tension. He held my hand. His little rucksack was on his knees, with some soft toys, cars and a computer which had his cartoons on it. We'd been driving for nearly four hours. In the end I put on a DVD to help pass the time. He was tired. It was a long journey for such a small boy.

The desert landscape became greener as we approached the Euphrates and its largest part, named Lake Assad by the regime. I didn't close my eyes once during the journey. My senses were on high alert and I was in a state of extreme vigilance.

The first signs of urban life began to appear around us, and I sat up straight. The suburbs looked poor, the houses and flats densely packed together. When we finally entered Raqqa itself, I was absorbed with taking in the city. My heart thudded. The first neighbourhoods we passed through were bustling and crowded, but not beautiful. Throngs of people spilled onto the road. Some streets were as packed as Paris during a protest march. Children were running everywhere. There were cars, motorbikes loaded with multiple passengers and street traders' carts, all jostling for space in the melee. Several buildings had visibly been bombed or were scarred by bullet marks, but most of all – pretty much everywhere – there were construction sites. Modern multi-storey apartment blocks all had balconies, with billboards hanging from them covered in Arabic writing I couldn't read as my knowledge of the language was still basic.

Some men were wearing Western clothes. These were Syrians. Others wore various military uniforms, in beige or camouflage, with scarves wrapped around their heads or necks, or were dressed Afghan style, with long tunics worn over baggy pants. These were mostly foreign fighters. There

were fewer women, long black silhouettes, indistinguisha-
ble from each other, parting the crowds like ghosts.

I was hungry for every detail, twisting my neck around to
see as much as possible. The car stopped in a bustling spot
and I recognised the boys coming towards us. Idriss and
Mohammed were accompanied by someone else I didn't
know, who was acting as their driver. I got out of the car to
meet them.

"Get in quickly," one of them said. "You can't walk about
like that here, Sophie. Hey, little guy!" This was to Hugo.

They took my case and hustled Hugo and me into their
car. We pulled out into the traffic.

"Didn't you bring a niqab?"

"No, I didn't know I had to."

"We'll go and buy you one straight away. It's pretty strict
here. You can't go out without being fully covered up."

In preparation for my arrival in the heart of the Islamic
State, I'd wrapped a shoulder length around scarf around
my face as soon as we reached the border. My head and neck
were completely covered. The boys seemed a bit nervous,
nevertheless.

We were happy to see each other, though. We looked at
each other, smiling and laughing. We didn't touch each
other, and I supposed that the rules governing behaviour
between men and women didn't allow it. But their delight
was genuine.

We stopped in front of a shop, which was a bit like an
indoor market. All it sold were the obligatory niqabs. Nothing
else. The shopkeepers had adapted to the situation.

Mohammed went inside and spent quite a long time
there while we waited, talking to Idriss just outside. He came
out carrying a bag, which he held out to me in the doorway.

"There you go. Put the veil on at least, we can sort the rest
out later."

I pulled on the veil, which was like a hooded cape, and the
boys finally calmed down. We entered into a quieter neighbourhood, which was more residential. The apartment

blocks were large, each with its own wrought iron gate. I didn't notice any street name, nor any road signs. I wondered if the Islamic State had taken them down, perhaps because they were named after officials from the Assad regime. I had no idea where we were. But I noticed some green spaces, small public gardens, like those where I'd imagined taking Hugo to play. We were getting closer, I told myself. The streets became even more peaceful, the traffic less congested. We slowed down and the boys parked the car.

I got out of the car, pleased to have arrived, when I saw her.

The woman was totally hidden beneath a black niqab; even her eyes were invisible, and her hands were gloved. She was walking by the side of a man wearing baggy trousers. They strolled along like any couple going for a stroll, nothing out of the ordinary, but when they passed us I realised that both were carrying a submachine gun on their back. I watched them walk past us, stunned.

It was our first day in Raqqa, "capital" of the Islamic State.

The lift didn't work; the power cuts were too frequent and you risked getting stuck, the boys explained as they carried our luggage up to the third floor. They opened the door of the apartment and gave me a set of keys, keeping a copy for themselves.

They showed us around, proud as peacocks of having found me such a splendid place to stay. They pointed out to me the details that seemed to them the most ostentatious signs of luxury: the mosaic on the walls, the two washing machines (although seeing the large basin next to them, I thought that hand-washing was more likely the norm), the Persian rugs, the enormous television. The apartment was luxurious. It was furnished in an Oriental style, a bit ornate and old-fashioned, which seemed to be the style here. I followed them, nodding my head, exhausted but also impressed. I never imagined I'd be entitled to stay anywhere like this.

Now we were inside they were more relaxed, and I found them jokey and affectionate, just like they used to be. Bit by bit, I also unwound.

"Why didn't you warn me about how crossing the border was going to be?"

"What were you expecting? The border with Turkey is closed, officially. The best places to cross over are always changing. It used to be by the side of Kills, now it's Urfa. It's not good to pass too much information over the internet, anyway."

Souleymane joined us, with some food. To make Hugo happy, he'd brought hamburgers and chips.

"You see? We don't want for anything here," they told me, very pleased with themselves.

Then they left us, so we could rest. Silence fell over the apartment. I walked slowly from one room to the another. I unfolded the clothes Mohammed had bought for me and laid them on the sofa. There was a long, very loose ankle-length robe with no collar and long sleeves, called an *abaya*. It was made from thick, black cloth, and I could wear my normal clothes underneath. Then there was a large cape, which went over the top of it. This covered the hair and neck, and hung down to the top of my thighs. This was what I'd put on in the car. It was designed to conceal the shape of the body as much as possible. Then I had to wear another layer of thick cloth, which covered the forehead and chin and reached down to the shoulders. This veil hid the face completely, including the eyes. An ingenious system of ties and Velcro held together two layers of fine cotton. With the first layer in place, you could still make out what was around you, as if you were looking at the world through a loosely woven cloth. With the second, you couldn't see anything unless you were in full daylight. You were plunged into darkness. It was obligatory to wear both veils.

The outfit was completed by black gloves. Feet should not be visible and women were not allowed to wear sandals, unless they were worn with opaque, black socks. Pensively, I gazed at this get-up. I knew I'd have to cover up, but never thought it would be to this degree. Each city has its own sounds, and from outside the window I could hear the hub-bub of the town. Suddenly, the last call to prayer filled the night, the imams' voices extinguishing all the other noises. I sighed and told myself, "when in Rome..." If I had to cover myself to be able to help the local people, I'd do it. To hell with my qualms. This would be my fancy dress for the few weeks I envisaged spending here.

Hugo was asleep, shattered. I walked from room to room silently. The apartment was a bit big for us. The boys told me they'd rented it from a Syrian family who'd gone to Turkey to get medical treatment for their son. I didn't know if this was the truth. It looked as if they'd left the place in a hurry. I found food in the fridge – opened jars, a bit past their sell-by date. The beds were not made, as if the occupants would be coming back in the evening after a day at work. There were still crumbs on the kitchen table.

The empty rooms seemed to emit a kind of dark energy, as if the murmur of interrupted conversations still lingered within them. I stood for a moment at the doors of the children's rooms. A boy and a girl had lived there. Their rooms were cheerful and tidy, full of educational games and soft toys crammed into chests. A revolving map of the stars, the names written in English, was pinned to the boy's wall.

They were everyday bedrooms, children's rooms with no trace of the war. My heart tightened at the thought of these kids, who'd perhaps been thrown out on the streets. I closed the door. A strange feeling took hold of me and the buzzing intensified in my head. I'd left Hugo in the small Eastern-style living room. There was another, fancier one with Western furniture. But it felt huge and inhospitable to me. In the small room, where Hugo was sleeping, foam mattresses were pushed up against the walls, serving as sofas. The centre of the room was occupied by a large, low table. On one side of the room there was a television. It was here that we'd spend most of our time, I imagined. The room was small and warm, thanks to the fabrics and cushions that adorned the mattresses. At one end of the low table, I made a pile of my son's colouring-in books and toy cars. We could eat at the other end. I put clean sheets on two of the mattresses. This would be the room we'd live in. A power cut plunged Raqqa abruptly into darkness. I snuggled up against Hugo and closed my eyes.

We didn't go out the next day, as we needed to acclimatise. Hugo played calmly in our little room while I kept myself busy with housework. I cleaned the cupboards from top to bottom, moving several things around so we could use the shelves for our clothes. I felt uncomfortable as I picked up a pile of blouses that must have belonged to the woman of the house, as though I was an intruder. If she came back, I wanted her to find everything in good order.

The kitchen led onto a terrace. I took Hugo onto it to look at the town. There was not a cloud in the immaculate, blue sky, but the winter light was pale. It was warm when the sun was shining, but as soon as it went down a pervasive chill spread through the air. Hugo was full of wonder when he discovered a birdcage with some canaries hopping around inside it. We took it out onto the terrace to give them some fresh air, and he sat crossed legged, admiring their colours and gracefulness. Aside from the Parisian pigeons, he'd never seen birds so close up. We watched them flutter around and listened to them sing. I wondered who'd fed them up until now. I filled their bowl with water and put some grains in the feeder.

The view from our balcony was magnificent. The town stretched out, as far as the eye could see, but it was not very high. Every town has its own colour and Raqqa, I would say, was yellow. There were patches of green here and there, but no fruit trees though. The boys' boasting made me smile. It was just like them to exaggerate.

I couldn't get a signal for my mobile phone. There was no landline in the apartment, nor any computer. The boys had advised me not to go out alone, not at first anyway. As soon as they came to see us, I'd ask them how I could communicate with the outside world. I carried on cleaning while I waited for them. I carefully closed all the bedroom doors. It was only in our little TV room that I felt comfortable.

In the hallway, I put some bags of clothes that Hugo had outgrown along with some medicines I'd brought from France, to give away. After lunch, which I made from whatever was at hand, Hugo wanted to watch TV but I couldn't get it to work.

"I'll play a film on your computer instead," I said.

"Ok, mama. I want to watch *Cars*."

"But you've already seen it ten times!"

I'd brought a hard disk full of films for Hugo and some serials for me. While he watched a cartoon, I listened out for what I could hear in our building. Before long, I heard a stampede of footsteps on the stairs and the happy, clear voices of children. I couldn't understand what they were saying, but when I heard them joined by the heavier footstep of an adult I imagined they were going outside for a walk. A woman's voice – their mother's, no doubt – was telling them to do something. Smiling, I imagined the universal command: "Shh, less noise, calm down children!"

The idea that a family was living in the same building reassured me. I knew so little about the place where we were staying, so had to squeeze out as much as I could from the smallest nuggets of information. I understood later that living among the Syrians part of the Islamic State's strategy; they spread themselves out in the city to escape the coalition's targeted bombing. There weren't any buildings occupied exclusively by foreign fighters. If the Syrian families were allowed to stay in their homes, it was because their presence protected the foreigners – like the boys and like me. They acted as a human shield.

"Are we going out for a walk, mama?" Hugo asked me, after the film.

"Not yet, not today. We'll go tomorrow."

I spent a good while playing "cars" with him, so he wouldn't get bored. I was his only friend here after all.

That evening, there were three rapid knocks at the door, followed by three slow ones. This was the signal I'd agreed with the boys. They'd told me not to open the door to anyone other than them. I hurried to the door. I was looking forward to some company, getting some news and having adults to talk to. Hugo was also excited to see them. They'd brought us something to eat. Chips again – I'd need to find out where to buy vegetables – and KFC style chicken. Hugo was delighted, of course. We went and sat in the living room and the five of us ate together. The boys were just as I'd always known them to be – protective and kind.

They told me that they had my passport, which they needed to keep for the time being, as a travel formality. I agreed to this, without knowing exactly what they meant by that.

"And for money? How will I go shopping and so on?"

"We told you, Sophie. Here, you don't need money. We're payed by the government, like all the foreigners. There's enough money for you and the little one. We'll take care of everything, don't worry."

I asked them what they spent their days doing.

"We work for the government," was their only response.

I didn't know if they were suspicious of me or if they were under orders not to say anything, but I sensed their reticence and didn't push them further. I thought that Souleymane, who'd always been a bit chubby, had lost weight and told myself that he must be doing some kind of physical work, or military training. But I didn't ask any more questions, as discretion seemed to be in order. They were dressed in tunics that hung over their baggy pants. They'd let their hair grow long, in the style adhered to by members of the Islamic State, while their beards were trimmed carefully as the Qur'an stipulated that facial hair should not touch the lips. I also noticed that they carried weapons, like all the foreigners. But in general, when they came to see me, they left them in their apartment.

The dinner was good fun. I noted that they were a little reticent when I gave them news of their families. They didn't engage with me, or ask any questions. They listened politely, rounding my stories off by saying "God be praised" or "God bless them," then changing the subject. I told myself it must be too painful a subject for them, and that they preferred to think of other things, but I felt ill at ease. Idriss didn't ask a single question about his mother which made me feel bad for his poor mum, who'd been in despair pining for her son since he left.

The boys suggested taking me to see the hospital the next day, where I hoped to work. I was worried about the language barrier and didn't know if I could be of any use.

"Almost no one here speaks Arabic. Only the Syrians and you shouldn't be dealing with them."

"Let's hope not for her sake anyway..."

They burst out laughing as if someone had told a particularly funny joke.

"The Syrians are gross. You've never seen such dirty people."

"They're morons, you'll see!" said Idriss, going even further. I couldn't believe my ears.

"What? This is like a French tourist on holiday abroad saying the local people are lazy and dirty. Can you hear yourselves?"

My words were met with jaded laughter.

"Seriously, you can't trust the Syrians," Idriss replied. "There are spies among them, Bashar's informers. And then, don't forget that you're a single woman here. There are men who'd take advantage of that. You know, before IS took control of the town, it was totally immoral here."

He told me that, as there was a military base located close to Raqqa, there had been brothels everywhere. It was utterly debauched, he said earnestly.

Mohammed changed the subject.

"Anyway, as far as the language goes, there's no need to worry. Souleymane and Idriss didn't speak good Arabic when they arrived and they haven't had any problem. Plenty of the foreign fighters here speak French. There are lots of French people, and others who come from Morocco or Algeria. And if not, then you'll be fine with English. It's a real Tower of Babel here, I'm telling you – except everyone understands each other."

I nodded my head. I'd soon find out.

The boys left us so I could put Hugo to bed. As the power had been cut again, there wasn't much I could do. It was my turn to rest now. I stretched myself out and fell immediately into a deep sleep.

8: The Baby Farm

The next day Hugo and I were woken up very early, firstly by a chorus of birdsong and immediately after by the call to prayer. I don't tend to pray regularly – at least not five times a day. I pray when I feel the need. So while the imam called the *adhan*,[6] I heated some milk for Hugo and made some coffee for myself. He stayed huddled under the covers; the temperature had fallen sharply during the night. I'd need to learn how to work the oil-fired heating system, which they had instead of electric radiators.

We ate our breakfast, clinging to each other in silence, watching as the sun came up and slowly flooded the room with rosy morning light. Then I got myself ready. For the first time I was going to put on what would be my uniform, and I couldn't quite bring myself to do it. I knew I'd have to be covered, but thought I'd be able to leave my face, my feet and my hands uncovered. But the niqab didn't allow this. I put on some light and comfortable clothes, with black tights. Then I put on my abaya. Then the cape. Hugo sat on the sofa, watching me attentively.

"Mummy's dressing up as batman," I said to him, to make him laugh.

"Can I dress up too?" Hugo's reply defused my unease.

I put on the hood and then the veil. The double layers over my eyes plunged me into darkness. I lifted one of them up – I'd see what would happen if I just wore the one. In the

---

6 The Muslim call to prayer, which summons believers before each of the five daily prayers.

meantime, I preferred to see where I was putting my feet. All I had to do now was put on my gloves. Then my flat shoes. I was ready. There were three light knocks at the door. The boys were there. Only Mohammed and Idriss had come. Souleymane was absent, as he was on the day we arrived. So off we went.

How strange it felt to walk on the street in my black veil! I felt as if I was hidden and yet the centre of attention at the same time. I had the illusion, however, of seeing without being seen, which was almost enjoyable, mixed up with the psychological and moral suffocation of feeling so confined and hemmed in. After several steps, I tripped and almost fell flat on my face.

"I'm taking this off – I can't see anything!"

"No, no Sophie, don't do that. The police are everywhere, you know."

I gave up, annoyed. Hugo was holding Mohammed's hand. I walked behind them, avidly taking in the streets – at least, what I could see of them through the fabric. It was a rich neighbourhood. The balconies were festooned with plants, the pavements were wide and clean. All the women were wearing the niqab. Some of them had been creative with the colour, but most were black. A lot of the men and some of the women were armed. They were carrying their rifles slung across their backs. In a low voice, I asked the boys questions.

"Who are these people?"

"Foreign fighters."

Under Daesh, all foreign fighters – whatever their position – were armed. On the other hand, very few Syrians were allowed to have weapons. Marching arrogantly down the middle of the pavement as if the street belonged to them, these foreigners looked more like an army of occupation than anything else. I noticed several vehicles with men dressed in black inside them. They were police cars, cruising slowly around town on the lookout.

"They're Daesh patrols – the militia. They check that everything is ok."

The boys seemed at home there. Twice they saluted some of the fighters in French, exchanging a few words with them. They didn't introduce me and no one spoke to me directly. In public, I did not exist. The boys left me at the entrance to the hospital. It was a maternity unit and only women were allowed inside. I went in alone, nervous and feeling unsure of myself. This was the whole reason for my trip, and I expected so much from the next few minutes.

The hospital was enormous, not very clean, and cluttered. The women inside had their faces uncovered. I quickly did the same and took a deep breath. Despite repeatedly telling myself I could put up with the niqab if that was what it took to do what I'd set my heart on, it was difficult. I'd convinced myself that they were just clothes and not my identity. Perhaps it was the same for the others, I thought as I watched the women coming and going in the hospital. I was reassured to see that they were pretty, wore make-up and were well-dressed. My niqab was a means of reaching the people that needed help.

I was welcomed by Umm Aïcha, a beautiful English woman. Her name signified she was the mother of Aïcha, her first born child. Here, I was Umm Hugo. I could see she was probably not a Muslim by birth and had converted. But she'd lived in Raqqa for a long time and had a senior position in the hospital. One of the young women whispered to me that she was one of the wives of the *emir*.

It was very difficult for women to understand how Daesh was organised, as they were kept away from decision making – or even simple information. An *emir* was a chief, and there was one of them for every province of the Islamic State. They were also known as *walis*. I never met Umm Aïcha's husband.

Umm Aïcha took me under her wing and showed me around the hospital. We spoke in English. Reassuring me about my lack of experience, she told me she wasn't a nurse and that she had learned "on the job". She wasn't particularly gentle with the patients, I noticed, when she gave them injections and performed other tasks.

What I discovered there left me with mixed feelings. I felt as though I'd visited a baby factory, the product of a sick mind, like a scene from a bad science fiction film. All the women, regardless of their diagnosis – or lack of it – gave birth by Ceasarean section. This was solely for the convenience of the medical staff. The conditions at the hospital were far from ideal and there was barely any supervision. There was no anaesthetist, for example, nor any kind of preliminary examination: everyone was simply given the same dose.

Throughout the wards, I saw drowsy young women struggling to come round from their anaesthetic, with their swaddled babies bawling in cots next to them. The medical care was very cheap for Syrians (it was free for foreigners), and most of the women who went there were extremely poor, from local tribes. Sometimes very young, they received few visits and little support. The sight of babies whimpering in every corner upset me greatly. The place was like a human livestock farm, with modern techniques but primitive aims. Syrians who had money preferred to go the private clinics which were still functioning, where there was better quality treatment.

Among the foreigners working in the hospital, there were Egyptians, Saudi Arabians and Tunisians. The main language spoken was Arabic, but I wasn't the only one who didn't speak it. The boys hadn't lied to me about that. Many of the foreigners, from France, Belgium or north Africa, spoke French. If not, we spoke in English.

I had a lot of reservations by the end of my visit. My first thought was that I wouldn't like to be treated there. Images came back to me from the days when I went with my mother to the clinic she managed. Those places were financed by Belgium, and the staff were devoted to their work, but most of all I remembered the Soviet metal beds, the crowded wards and the old equipment. I recognised the thick, heavy woollen blankets covering the sleeping women here. They were like the ones in Yaoundé, but here they were old and not washed frequently enough. I noticed traces of dried blood or vomit on some of them. It was more like a field hospital run on a shoestring than a facility worthy of a capital city. Medical standards were low. There were no blood tests for the women, neither for AIDS nor for hepatitis. Basic rules of hygiene were not respected; I saw half-full feeding bottles lying around everywhere, left all afternoon, the curdled milk providing an ideal breeding ground for bacteria. Clouds of flies buzzed around us.

On my way out, I picked up Hugo who I'd left at the nurse's station with his little computer. His cartoon was over and he was ready to leave. *"Ma'as salam"*, he said conscientiously, prompting laughter from the women who'd been teaching him some Arabic words. He ran to join me.

I was feeling anxious as we left the hospital. We were walking back to the apartment alone; the boys had warned me they couldn't pick us up as they'd be at work. They said there shouldn't be any problem for me to walk back in the daytime, so long as I was with Hugo and correctly veiled. I had memorised the way. We passed by a small square I'd noticed on the way to the hospital and stopped there. I sat on a bench and watched Hugo play with the other children. I had to encourage him a bit, but after a moment of shyness his confidence returned, and he joined the little group.

It made me happy to see him laugh and letting himself go. As when I first arrived in Raqqa, I was surprised at the number of children I saw out in the streets and parks during the day. They were everywhere. When I asked the boys about it that evening, they explained to me that all the schools had been closed by Daesh, which was working to bring the curriculum into line with the Quranic principles established by the Caliphate. The children had been left to their own devices while waiting for the new system to be created. There were some secret schools, organised by groups of parents. Other families just taught their children at home themselves.

The women sitting on the benches weren't speaking to each other, keeping themselves to themselves. In my case, it was because I didn't speak Arabic. But perhaps they didn't either? How would I know?

That night, the boys asked me about my day. I told them what I'd seen and that, in my opinion, the maternity ward was in a deplorable state.

"Sophie, you have to change your attitude. You think too much like a French person."

I nearly choked on my kebab.

"How can you say that? You've never even put one foot in Africa! *I* grew up in Cameroon. Who's the French person here?"

Idriss was not happy.

"You're totally prejudiced in how you see things."

"You're the one full of preconceived ideas. You think I'm fine with dirt because I'm African? My mother was a head nurse and I can tell you she would not have approved of anything I saw today – and she was African, 100% Cameroonian!"

"Woah, woah," Mohammed broke in, soothingly. He always played the part of the "good cop".

"Let's not argue. Sophie is discovering new things, she needs to get used to them and we need to give her a bit of time."

I didn't like his paternal tone, but I let it go. It was true that I didn't want to argue with them. I didn't know anyone else there. And I liked them, these boys.

Over the next few days, I volunteered part-time at the hospital. Hugo played and filled in his colouring books at the nurses' station, where the women took turns looking after him. Several of them spoke French, so communicating wasn't difficult. Not being medically trained, I was grateful to do what I could: to bring a glass of water to the young mother of a new-born, to gather up half-finished babies' bottles, or to comfort a young girl having a particularly hard time as she came round from her anaesthetic.

Little by little, I started to understand the different strata of society in Raqqa. At the top of the pyramid were the foreigners. Mostly men, along with some women, they were from all over the world. In the hospital I met women who'd come from North Africa, West Africa and Australia. Most had come to join their husbands, others had arrived together as a couple. I didn't tell anyone I'd come on my own as this wasn't the usual situation, and I didn't want to arouse any curiosity. Although I didn't like the idea of it, the boys were my legal guardians. They'd had to request a certificate to allow them accompany me on the street.

Within the foreign population, there were important distinctions. There were the fighters, the mujaheddin. Without any real uniform, they generally bought their own weapons. They spent their days at training centres when they weren't taking part in active combat.

I didn't know what the others did, which posts they filled in Daesh's organisational structure. I had the impression that mainly they were there to hold the town and intimidate the population. There was an subtle hierarchy among them. One day, in the market, the boys pointed out a young man to me with evident respect. He was Nicolas, a French convert, who was known for his propaganda videos. The Islamic State's police force patrolled menacingly throughout the town.

Below the foreigners were the Syrians. Among them, those who'd declared allegiance to Daesh were obviously in a better situation than the others. Supporters of the President were mercilessly hunted down and killed, as were those of the Free Syrian Army – with whom Daesh had, at one time, formed an opportunistic alliance. At the bottom of the pile were the poorest of the Syrians – the little people who stayed quiet and kept their heads down, hoping things would work out in the end. Skin colour influenced social status: dark skinned Syrians were on the lowest rung of the ladder, while those with fairer complexions made up the bourgeoisie. In the hospital, the pretty young girls from the tribes who came to give birth all had very dark skin. Confronted with this caste system, with its untouchables and ruling class, I felt like I was in India.

The foreigners were virulently contemptuous of the Syrians. The prejudices I'd heard from the boys were widespread: the Syrians were dirty, lazy, they were bad Muslims who loved nothing more than smoking the *shisha*[7] (which was now punishable by prison – or worse, if a woman was present) and drinking alcohol. They were bad Muslims, who needed re-educating. In the streets, the foreign fighters brutally exerted their authority. They didn't queue up in the shops and they'd shove the Syrians on the pavement out of their way. Who would answer back to an armed man? The Syrians would lower their heads and move aside.

All this shocked me and made me uncomfortable. I hadn't come here to replay colonialism, even less as a colonialist. I tried to explain my uneasiness to the boys, who

---

7   A glass-bottomed water pipe in which fruit-flavoured tobacco is covered with foil and roasted with charcoal.

didn't understand. I was rapidly developing a loathing for these foreigners, who saw themselves as superior. I watched this army of occupation, these arrogant men patrolling the streets of the town while the civilians came and went, pretending not to see them. "This," I thought, "is like the 3rd Reich in Paris. They're like the colonialists in Cameroon, the settlers and the Native Americans." I was utterly repulsed at the thought of being part of this system.

It was the same at the hospital. I didn't understand how the women could be so brutal or indifferent to the young girls they were supposed to be helping. I saw one of the foreign volunteers insult a young Syrian woman, sobbing as she woke from her anaesthetic in a terrible state. It reminded me of an internship I'd done at an old people's home before finding my first job. Here too, the staff behaved as if they were superior. The nurses and volunteers all believed themselves to be better than these young Syrian women. They believed themselves to be *muhajirs*, those who had left their non-Muslim countries for a Muslim land, and the most Muslim one at that. They referred to it as making the *hijra*[8] and believed themselves to be the elite.

Every night, at least two of the boys would join Hugo and I for dinner. Hugo was always happy to see them, as he was missing male company. Big kids themselves, they'd happily play with him, calling him their "little man". Mohammed suggested taking Hugo with him during the day, so I could work without having to worry about him, but I didn't want to be separated from my son. I said no.

In privacy of the apartment I'd uncover my face, but they insisted that I kept my hair covered up. Before entering, they'd warn me they were there with the pre-arranged signal. I didn't know anyone else in the building, but I knew there were families there – I could guess this from seeing shoes of

---

8   *Hijra* refers to the journey made by the Prophet Mohammed in 622 AD from Mecca to Medina, to escape persecution. It marks the beginning of Islam as a community in which spiritual and earthly life were completely integrated.

different sizes outside some of the front doors. Sometimes I heard footsteps and children's voices, but generally it was silent. People stayed in their homes. No one trusted anyone.

The boys had told me that there was a Christian family living on the first floor. I clung to this, as if the presence of people from other religions was proof of possible tolerance. Then I learned that they had to pay a special tax in order to be given the same rights as the Muslims.

Some of the women were armed, usually the Chechens, the boys told me; while Western women were considered as delicate objects in need of protection, the Chechens were as hard as nails. Among the Syrian women, there were some who were very attracted to the jihadists. They'd line their eyes with kohl and not cover them up. One time, while we were walking together on the street, one of them gave Idris a flirty look. He preened himself.

"You see, Sophie, we can have any woman we want here!"

It was the reaction of the boy he'd been before: full of himself, but awestruck at the same time. He made me laugh. When I wanted to make them happy, I'd call them by their *kunya*, the nicknames they'd chosen. Demonstrating their lack of sophistication, Idriss and Mohammed had chosen the same one: "Al Taleb." To differentiate between the two, one was "Al Taleb from Burkina" and the other, "Al Taleb from Morocco." They really were kids, I thought to myself.

I tried to explain to them what I was feeling, but they wouldn't accept my criticisms. They had less and less objectivity about the Islamic State.

"We're at war, Sophie. The behaviour of the fighters in the baker's shop is not a priority. You don't understand – the enemy is hidden among the population. We can't trust anyone."

"Yes, but I came here to help and I've ended up finding myself taking part in oppressing people. We're not on the right side."

"My sister, you see everything through your Western glasses. You're influenced by propaganda. Things are more complicated than you know."

My sister...Here, all the members of the Islamic State called each other "brother" and "sister". I didn't want to be part of their family.

Our arguments became more and more frequent. They disapproved of Hugo's films. They thought that he should watch cartoons in Arabic, to get used to the language and the culture. Then there was music. Music was forbidden. I burst out laughing.

"Is this the ex-rapper who's saying this? Have you forgotten where you came from?" Like many young guys from housing estates, the three of them had formed a rap group when they were teenagers.

"And do you have a problem with what I'm watching?" I was midway through the series, *Orange is the New Black*, the story of women prisoners whose conduct left something to be desired according to Quranic principles: they smoked, drank, had lesbian sex...We ended up joking, but I felt that we were growing further and further apart.

I was learning the rules that governed life under the Islamic State, the ones they'd carefully refrained from telling me. I never suspected that I wouldn't be able go out alone, take a taxi or that I would need a guardian. They'd convinced me that I could go there without being part of the Islamic State group. They'd said that it was possible to live a Western life, which was manifestly impossible. Little by little, the thought that they'd deliberately lied to me began to take shape.

10: The Awakening

By 8pm, it was pitch black. Hugo and I played with torches in our bedroom after eating dinner under a camping lantern. He fell asleep cuddled up against me. Listening to his deep breaths and the little sounds he made in his sleep, I started thinking. I felt confused. Since I arrived, I'd felt in a state of torpor, which I attributed to the tiredness from the journey. Aside from arguments with the boys, which were happening more and more often, I spoke little and kept my own counsel. I was finding it difficult to think clearly.

There was no open telecommunications network in Syria. You had to buy gigabytes of credit in cybercafés, some of which were controlled by the Islamic State. I'd gone and got the wifi code from a neighbouring one; their coverage reached as far as the apartment, so I could communicate without going outside.

Two or three days after we arrived, I made contact with Julien again. I pretended we'd arrived safely in Turkey and that I'd started my volunteer work. The communications were very bad; the line kept cutting out, so I preferred writing to him. I sent him news about Hugo and told him how I was spending my days, changing a few details since I'd told him I was in an orphanage, not a maternity unit. The boys knew I was in touch with my husband and they'd emphasised that I shouldn't give out too much information. I promised I wouldn't. It wasn't forbidden to communicate with people in France. On the contrary, in fact. This was how they'd persuaded me to come, and IS needed fresh meat – cannon fodder, and women for the fighters. In turn, each new follower was likely to spread positive news about life in Raqqa, which was Daesh's policy. Communications were controlled, but not forbidden.

Julien's messages were affectionate and concerned. He never scolded me, but tried to get closer to me instead. It was strange having conversations about the future of our love, and our chances of overcoming the crisis that had separated us while – unknown to him – I was in Raqqa. During these discussions, or in our email exchanges, Julien was very sweet. Little by little, he restored my faith in our history together. He talked about us, how we met and the early days of our relationship. He sent me photos, some of which gave me a shock; it was as if I'd forgotten their existence. I realised that I missed him. I started wanting to go home.

"Sophie, I'd like to know where exactly you are with Hugo, to show me some places, so I know you're ok." I lied and was vague, but sent him photos of Hugo and me to reassure him. He said that I'd lost weight and looked tired.

He told me that my sister had fallen ill, which upset me. Without spelling it out, he implied that it was anxiety about Hugo and me that had worn her down. We'd only left ten days ago, but the vagueness of my plans had unsettled them all. I also imagined that they knew I'd resigned from my job, even if Julien didn't bring it up. I felt guilty I'd caused so much worry.

I also received some kind, warm messages through Facebook from a former colleague, saying that they'd been really sorry to see me go from the community centre and missed me. She reminded me of some of the crazy situations we'd faced together, which made me laugh. I shivered. When I spoke with Julien, or chatted with my colleague, I had moments of clarity. Suddenly my old life would seem rich and full, even if it hadn't been perfect, and I'd feel as if everything was back as it was. Then we'd hang up and there I was again; alone in Raqqa, uncertain, confused and mixed-up.

I often took Hugo to the park opposite the house. One day, while I was watching him play, a woman approached me and gestured to Hugo with her gloved hand.

"He's cute. How old is he?" she asked, in poor English.

"Four years."

It was impossible to know what she looked like. I could barely see her eyes behind the veil. She had several children with her, who let Hugo join in with their games. She nodded her head and gave a timid laugh. The conversation stopped there. She lived in the same building as me, in the top floor apartment, but I wouldn't recognise her if I saw her there.

Julien wrote to me every day, sometimes several times a day. In his last email, I discovered a photo I didn't remember. I was pregnant with Hugo, posing in profile with an enormous smile. My face, which was turned towards the camera, towards Julien, shone with happiness. I was transfixed. It was as though I'd never seen this seen this picture before.

"It was your favourite photo," Julien wrote. I don't know how I could have forgotten it.

It was as if a part of my life emerged from the mist when I saw this image. The places I'd left behind me took shape again and my memories drifted back. With each message from Julien, they grew sharper. For the first time, I asked myself, incredulously, whether I'd been brainwashed. But it was impossible. How could three guys – at least ten years my junior – have manipulated me? They weren't even that smart. I would have thought that to turn someone's head in this way it would take charisma, skill and a high level of intelligence. In my eyes, they had none of these qualities. Perhaps it was the depression, I thought, that had diminished my ability to think clearly.

I was at the hospital when everything finally clicked into place. So many things had happened since I'd arrived that it felt as if I'd been there for months. It was hard to believe I'd only been there for ten days or so. That day, I was walking through the maternity ward carrying some clean sheets when I saw a new-born baby, screaming its head off. The bed next to the cot was empty. I found a nurse and asked why the baby had been left alone.

"The mother died during childbirth," she told me, without batting an eyelid.

"What?"

"It happens." She shrugged.

"And the baby?"

"The family have been informed and are coming to take the baby. The mother was from a village and they won't get here before the evening."

She went on her way, leaving me with my legs trembling and mouth hanging open. The baby went on howling from the cot. The distress and loneliness were unbearable to behold. Automatically, I stepped forward and scooped the child up into my arms. She was a girl. I held her close to me and began humming the lullabies which used to calm Hugo down when he was small, the same ones that my mother used to sing to me. The baby quietened down a bit as I rocked her. But this little orphan had broken my heart. I felt a powerful wave, thick and black, engulf me. The light was sucked out from the world, along with the desire to live and be happy, and there was only the baby and myself holding onto each other, alone.

Suddenly, if I was looking from afar, I saw myself standing in this awful ward full of young, pregnant women, holding a tiny orphan to my heart, in a city under occupation in a country at war. The realisation was so forceful that my legs gave way. I fell into a wheelchair, still holding the baby against me. A while later, an older woman with only her hair covered (a privilege accorded with age) stepped hesitantly into the clinic. She walked along the corridors until she reached the ward where I was. Her eyes were dry, but there was a trace of bitterness in the lines around her mouth. She seemed resigned. She gently took the baby, wrapped her in a dirty shawl and left without a backwards glance.

When I arrived back at the apartment, I looked around me and suddenly felt like I was seeing clearly again. The large winter sun shone over Raqqa, over the women in black, the fighters and the Syrians, living under occupation. What the hell was I doing there? That evening, I called Julien. My throat felt tight.

"Sophie, I want you to come home. I miss you and I miss Hugo. It's time, now."

His voice was soft and my throat tightened even more.

"I'm going to come back, Julien. I promise."

After putting Hugo to bed, I stayed awake for a long time, staring into space. Images raced through my mind. The trip Julien and I made to Bolivia. We'd travelled across the country by train, through vast forests. The account a friend of mine from the community centre had given of working in a Palestinian orphanage one summer. My nieces rehearsing a musical comedy, both of them sharing the leading role. My sister coming home triumphantly from the market. Hugo as a baby, lying on his father's stomach, both of them fast asleep on the sofa. I felt at peace, as though I had found what I was looking for.

I needed to go home.

11: "I want to go home"

The next day, I announced that I wanted to go home. It was the beginning of March and I'd been there for two weeks. The boys were stunned.

"But why? Why so soon?"

"My family isn't happy. They're worried."

"Hold on, there's no need to rush things. Show them you're happy and that'll reassure them. Look how we did it."

I stared at them, incredulous.

"You think your families were reassured? Mohammed, your mother tried to kill herself!"

The boys shook their heads as if I didn't want to understand.

"It's difficult for the families, but you have to be strong. A lot of people give up because of them. You can't be weak."

"Ok, but it's different for me – I have to go back in 15 days anyway. It doesn't change anything."

They didn't reply.

"Can you find out if it's possible?"

"Sure we'll find out, Sophie," promised Mohammed, always keen to avoid conflict.

"Do you want us to come with you to the hospital?" asked Idriss.

"I'm never going back there," I replied, curtly. They exchanged looks, but didn't insist I should go. They left for work, leaving Hugo and me in the flat.

From that day, I raised the subject every time they came to the apartment.

"Have you asked anyone about my return? Who do you need to ask? Is there any news?"

They told me to be patient, that it was being dealt with. At the same time, they tried to convince me to stay.

"What are you afraid of? There aren't any bombs, there's no danger. Do you have an apartment like this in France?"

Their voices would rise, but they never became angry. Yet something told me leaving wasn't going to be as easy as I thought.

On 6th March, it was my birthday. They didn't say anything about it, as celebrating birthdays wasn't a Muslim tradition. But I received many kind messages through the internet, which brought tears to my eyes. Julien told me that my sister was beside herself with worry on my behalf, which upset me. That evening I insisted to the boys I had to go home. I told them my sister was ill in an attempt to persuade them. They knew I was an orphan, and that she'd brought me up. I thought that they'd give in. I wasn't afraid, I was just impatient. I didn't want to wait another 15 days.

I was still so naïve.

Julien and I spoke every day, but never for too long so as to save on phone credit. I thought a lot about our relationship. I realised that I had been looking for a father figure in him, and that this must have been a heavy weight to bear. As we talked, I was getting to know him again. I felt ready, now, to begin a relationship with him that was more well-balanced. I told myself it was possible to start again.

I kept on asking the boys whether they'd spoken to anyone about my return to France. "It makes no difference," I said to them, "whether I go back now or in two weeks." The boys dodged the question, never giving a straight answer. Hugo and I went out very little. In my head, we'd already left Raqqa.

Once again, I tackled them. This time I told them that my sister had been hospitalised.

"Have you said where you are?"

"No, of course not. But she's really ill. You know that she brought me up – I can't leave her like this."

"There are sacrifices you have to make..."

Their idiotic stubbornness made me furious. I just couldn't get through to them.

"Listen, you told me that I could come for a few weeks to see what it was like. So I did. Now I have to go back. I can't leave my family like this."

"Ok Sophie, ok. We'll see,' said Mohammed. "But be patient, because we'll need to contact the Emir and it's complicated, you know?"

"It didn't seem so complicated when you wanted me to come out here!"

"That was different. You know that we're at war. We have to make sure that you're not going to give away any sensitive information."

"What could I give away? I don't know anything! I haven't even told my family I'm in Syria..."

"Ok, ok. Just give us a bit of time."

Hugo refused to hug them when they left. He'd become more and more clingy with me. He didn't say anything, but his anxiety showed by how close he stuck to me. I noted that he was less friendly with the boys – he even refused to high five Idriss one evening, something he used to love doing. Idriss turned away, looking vexed. Relations with the boys were deteriorating.

The days went by. Each evening, I asked them where they were at with the question of our departure, taking care not to raise my voice and upset Hugo. For their part, they did their best to convince me to change my mind.

"Why can't you try again, Sophie? You need to show willing..."

"I don't care about being 'willing'! Don't make me lose my temper. Keep your word, Idriss! Idriss, listen to me. It's me, Sophie, you're talking to, Idriss." I said his name, repeating it, as if by doing so it would bring back the good kid I knew.

It didn't work, because he no longer existed. I still didn't understand that.

12: Prisoner

Sometime in the afternoon on the 15th or 16th March, Idriss and Mohammed rapped on the door, using the special knock we'd agreed. I looked around for my headscarf. They came in and looked at me, their faces grim and unsmiling.

"Tell us who's trying to get you to leave."

Once more, I started talking to them about my sister who was ill.

"Hand over your phone. We need to see what you've been telling people."

"I haven't said anything! I've told you, no one even knows I'm in Syria."

I was getting angry because I was afraid. This time, I had the feeling that they wanted to stop me leaving. It wasn't that they were just disappointed I wanted to go back to France. It was more than that, it was a categorical refusal. I now understood that they weren't going to let me leave. I kept talking to them as I usually did, arguing with them as though I was their older sister, but I had the sense that something had changed.

We were in the living room while Hugo was playing in the small bedroom. The conversation dried up. There was no common ground between us anymore. The two of them got up and walked towards the front door. I waited until I heard it close, then looked around for my phone. I'd left it on a small round table.

It was no longer there. The boys were my enemies now. I was terrified.

They came back the next day and demanded I give them my key.

"Why? You have a copy and I can't go out alone anyway."

"Exactly. You won't need it now you don't want to work anymore. You have no need to go outside."

There was nothing I could do. And just like that, we were locked up like prisoners. I cursed my stupidity. From that day on, every time the boys came to the apartment (knocking in the special way, to make sure I'd always be properly covered up), Hugo would run to my side like a loyal soldier and fix them with a baleful stare.

"Leave my mama alone!" he cried out at Idriss, who didn't respond.

The days when the boys would call him "little man" were over. There were no more games, no more playing with him and his toy cars. I decided to go on hunger strike immediately to give them something to think about. I'd make them feel sorry for me – they wouldn't let me die.

I skipped dinner on the first night of my strike. Strangely, I had never been so hungry as that evening. The next day I had only drank tea at breakfast. At midday, the smell of the purée I gave to Hugo made my stomach rumble violently, but I felt fine. I'd fasted before to detox – it was something I'd been doing from time to time since adolescence. It made me feel good, as if I'd been cleansed. I'd also fasted for Ramadan the year before, but I'd never fasted entirely for longer than two days. I braced myself.

A bit of pressure should be enough to bring them round, I told myself. That was how things had worked with them before – they'd back down and say, "It's ok Sophie, we were only joking." When I heard them speak in inner city slang, when I heard them say "Yo, whaddup?" it calmed me down. They weren't really fanatic terrorists, just kids from the estates. Everything would be fine.

I didn't understand that they were in the middle of the process of transformation. They were between two states, but had began shedding their skins. The next day, I told them I needed to go shopping.

"I need to go out."

"You can't go out alone."

"There's something I need to buy."

"Tell us and we'll bring it for you."

"Ok then, I need some tampons."

Mohammed's face reddened. For them, periods were unclean. A woman could not pray during her menstrual cycle, touch a Qur'an or have sexual relations. The boys were embarrassed. They spoke rapidly with each other, then turned to me.

"You can go tomorrow. But Hugo will stay here."

"I'm not going anywhere without my son."

"Well, you'll just have to manage without then."

I realised I wasn't going to be able to make them budge, and now I felt really scared. What if they kidnapped Hugo? Or me?

"You're crazy. He's just a four-year old – he needs to go outside. It's not healthy for him to be inside all the time."

"It's up to you. If you come to your senses, it won't be like that."

"If 'coming to my senses' means staying in Syria, then there's no chance of that. You promised that I could go back. You're not keeping your word"

The same discussion, over and over again.

The next day, I went to the market a few blocks away. I had to move fast. They'd finally allowed Hugo to come with me, but he slowed me down and I was afraid I wouldn't have time for what I'd planned. I walked as fast as was possible for Hugo to keep up with me. I stopped at the cybercafé, hurried down the few steps to the shop and asked to make a phone-call.

Luckily, Julien picked up on the first ring. I spoke quickly and very quietly. The line kept breaking up, and there were French speakers everywhere around us. I couldn't risk one of them overhearing me.

"Julien, we're in Syria and they won't let us go. Hugo's fine, but you have to get us out of here." From thousands of miles away, I could feel his terror – and anger.

"Where are you?"

"Raqqa. Please help us."

"Have they hurt you?"

"No. You have to tell someone – they won't let us go!"

The line cut. I tried calling back, but couldn't get through again. I left, shaking, and headed back to the house, making a detour to the pharmacy on the way. I looked around me in the street, scared that the boys might have seen me. I climbed the stairs as fast as I could and tapped out the special knock when I reached the apartment. "It's me, Sophie," I whispered through the door. Idriss opened it.

That evening, when the boys brought us some food for dinner, Idriss showed me a photo he'd taken without my knowledge on his phone with a mocking smile: Hugo, posing with a submachine gun. What I didn't know was that he would send it to Julien. Thousands of miles away, out of his mind with worry, my husband would receive a picture of his four-year-old son proudly showing off a weapon almost as big as himself.

I was aggressive with the boys when they came to the flat now, following them from room to room like a woman possessed, insisting that Hugo should be allowed out.

"He's just a little boy! You can't keep him locked up like this," I was crying from the worry of it all.

"That's up to you, Sophie."

"You promised!"

"Let him come to the mosque with us."

"Not on my life. He's staying with me. Let us go to the park at least."

They shook their heads, resolute. It was no use.

The days rolled on. The weather grew colder and the nights were frosty sometimes. I left the heating on all the time in our small room. The smell of oil it emitted filled the air, clinging to our clothes and hair. I had dreams sometimes in which we were dying from carbon monoxide poisoning, but it was too cold not to keep it burning. The rest of the flat was too big to heat, and it was freezing. Every afternoon when the weather was pleasant, Hugo and I would carry the birds in their cage on to the balcony, so they could get some air. The moment they came into the light, they would start to sing. As I sat telling Hugo stories, I dreamed of releasing the birds from their cage and letting them do what we could not – claim back their freedom and fly away, far from Syria.

Our life was monotonous, but Hugo never complained. Once or twice he looked at the trees in the garden where he wanted to play and said sadly, "I'd love to go for a walk." That was all. When he heard footsteps on the stairs and the voices of children, he froze and listened with his entire being.

More days passed with the same weary sluggishness, each identical to the last. I tried to distract Hugo with stories. Fortunately, he never got bored when I rehashed the same tales. We made up Chinese shadow plays on the wall. We watched cartoons. It felt as though we were holding our breath. A week passed. Then another. One day, I cornered the boys near to the front door and whispered to them, in tears. "My little boy will go crazy like this. He needs to go out. I'm begging you!" I gasped.

But nothing touched them. There was no emotion, no hesitation in the way they looked at me. They had no doubts.

"You bastards! You've become monsters!" My voice rose in spite of myself.

"Mama?" Hugo's worried voice floated down the corridor.

I wiped the tears from my face before turning around. He was there, behind me, watchful and suspicious, ready to defend me.

"Is everything ok, mama?"

"I'm fine, darling. Mama's fine."

I heard the door close behind me.

We'd been locked up for three weeks. I felt like I was going crazy, like an insect flying against a window pane. The boys came every evening, or every couple of evenings, to bring us food. Even when they came every other day I didn't miss what they brought because by now I'd stopped eating entirely. There was always enough for Hugo. I cooked him rice and tuna, seasoned with ketchup, but I ate nothing myself.

Since they wouldn't listen to me, they needed to see me so they'd understand I was serious. After the first few days, I didn't find it so hard. I was no longer hungry, even when I fed my son. Food no longer bothered me. I felt that I was growing weaker, though – I was dizzy when I stood up now. I knew I'd lost weight because I'd had to make two more holes in my belt already. But the boys didn't react. In fact, I found them more and more indifferent.

Every time as they came to the apartment, I confronted them straight away. I wasn't afraid now. They acted like men, but I knew they were still kids, really. Rude, cocky kids and maybe dangerous too, but I still felt I had a kind of maternal power over them.

"Give me back my mobile phone and my passport." Every evening began like this. I harassed them, I argued with them, I insisted they kept their word. I followed them from one end of the apartment to the other, pulling apart the arguments with which the supposedly paradisiacal Islamic State had used to manipulate and blind them. In vain.

I decided upon a new tactic and told them I was ill. I wasn't lying; I had an ovarian cyst that I'd decided not to have operated on before leaving for Syria, as the surgery carried a risk of infertility. Idriss sneered when I told him.

"Awww...are you ill, like your sister? You're nothing but a liar."

"What?"

"Your sister was never in hospital. We checked."

"But she really was ill. I said she was in hospital because that was what I understood. Perhaps she's been discharged since? Believe me, I'm telling you the truth. I was going to have the operation before leaving France. I have to be treated or I'll no longer be able to have children."

I could see I hadn't convinced him.

"I need to buy more tampons."

"Oh yeah? Isn't that a bit soon?"

"That's how my cycle goes. You can go yourself if you prefer."

I hadn't had a period for a while, not since I stopped eating. But he wasn't to know that.

This time, when I went downstairs to go to the souq, I stopped at the door of the Christian family on the first floor. I was afraid of being overheard in the cybercafé; there were spies everywhere. I knocked at the door. A woman opened, looking apprehensive. In English, I explained that I'd lost my mobile phone and needed to make a call. I was their neighbour from upstairs. I could see she didn't trust me – she looked behind me at the stairs, as if expecting an ambush.

But she let me come inside and use her phone – perhaps because she didn't dare refuse anything to a foreigner for fear of the consequences. I called Julien. Once again, he answered after the first ring. He must have been waiting constantly for me to call. I whispered quickly, but he didn't understand what I was saying and I had to repeat everything several times. The woman stared at me, and I hoped she didn't speak French. I asked him to send a medical certificate. A friend of his parents was a doctor. He needed to attest that I suffered from a gynaecological illness which needed a particular type of treatment. It should be sufficiently serious that I would need to leave Syria on the grounds of ill health. I clung to this hope.

From this moment, I insisted that the boys make enquiries. I told them that my doctor could send medical information, and that I needed to check my email account. But we couldn't connect to the network as the connection was too weak. I learned later that they called Julien for confirmation of my condition. But – just like the story with my sister – it didn't work. Nothing worked.

My relationship with the boys was getting worse and worse. They scolded me for not praying, treating me like an unbeliever. I bombarded them with furious insults. "Baghdadi doesn't give a damn about you," I told them. "You're the idiots, you assholes!" They threatened that I'd be stoned to death or shot. Sometimes I'd try again to reason with them.

"Let Hugo go and I'll do what you want. Take him to the border and his dad can come and get him."

"We don't speak to infidels."

"I have Muslim friends – I can ask them to come and get him. After that, I'll make no more problems."

"You want to give up your son? What kind of mother are you, who'd abandon her kid?"

Aside from these clashes, which had grown more and more harsh, life was very quiet for Hugo and I. We woke at sunrise, at the time of the first prayer, and I made him breakfast. After that we usually went back to bed for a bit. Sometimes, Hugo fell asleep again. If not, we'd watch films under the covers. I barely slept any more. I could hardly force myself to smile anymore, to keep going. Hugo sensed my mood and stayed close to me at all times. We kept busy as best we could. We read, he leafed through his comic books and I told him stories. We took the canaries onto the balcony. We looked into the horizon. I was sure I could see Turkey, far away across the mountains in the distance. We looked up at the birds circling over the town, imagining what it must be like to fly. Hugo listened to the sound of children playing downstairs, but he no longer begged me to go outside. Everything around us felt hostile now.

I had always been very protective of my son and without doubt had treated him like a baby. Now I was beginning to feel there was no way out, and that I might die there. It was now three weeks since I'd eaten. I didn't know how we could get out of this situation. I was terrified that if I died, the boys would get their hands on my little boy. He was so young that it would be easy to brainwash him. They'd make him into a monster.

So I tried, while I still had time, to leave him with an imprint of memories and knowledge that couldn't be erased. I told him that his father loved him. I told him always to be kind to women. He promised he would be and hugged me, stroking my cheeks to comfort me.

"Are you ok, mama?" he'd ask, thirty times a day. I whispered back words of love and reassurance, words that would help him withstand anything they could to do to him.

I had to try something before my energy ran out completely. In my head, I went through different escape plans over and over again. Perhaps we could get onto the roof of the building next door from the balcony. I couldn't see enough from here, but I imagined that we could find a way to the staircase inside. If not, we could jump down from balcony to balcony, to the street. But it was too risky at such a height. If Hugo fell, he'd die. And then, even if we made it onto the street, where would we go? How would we escape? Who could we ask for help?

I thought about starting a fire in the flat. The boys would have to let us out, and we could make a run for it. Sometimes I thought about throwing myself, naked, from the balcony. I'd just be sorry not to see their faces when they had to pick up the body of a naked woman. This would be the final solution, for when there was no hope left.

Not eating made everything hazy; there were times when I seemed to be hallucinating and losing myself in daydreams, from which only Hugo's voice asking *are you ok, mama?* could pull me back.

"Yes, darling," I'd tell him. "I'm fine."

One day, the boys were at the apartment when the call to prayer came and they made their ablutions in the flat. They had to put down their weapons as they washed themselves, and I thought about grabbing a gun and shooting them, riddling the three of them with bullets. Then Hugo and I would run. I had to shake myself to come out of this fantasy. I had to do something soon, or I'd go crazy. But more often, they didn't come inside when they brought our food now.

I spent a long time with my ear stuck to the front door, listening to the sounds of the building. I didn't know what good it would do, but I told myself that if we managed to escape it could be useful. I had a feeling that the Christian woman wouldn't help us. But I often thought about the other Syrian woman in the building, the one who had approached me and spoken in English. The one who walked past my door every day with her children.

During prayer times, everything stopped. The stairwell was almost always deserted. I took note of everything, storing the information up carefully in my head. I'd only get one chance, and I couldn't afford to mess it up.

Night fell over the city; once again there was a power cut. The time went so slowly, it felt like it had stopped. I was building a bubble for the two of us, so we could stay strong. I didn't want to think of the suffering I'd caused to everyone waiting for me at home. I kept myself focused on one goal – to get Hugo out of there. I was living only for my son. If I could only find a way to keep him safe, I'd be happy to let myself die. I had a strange feeling of having truly become a mother, as if I was experiencing the bond for the first time in its utmost purity: there was nothing I would not do for him.

That evening, Idriss came in alone. He held up his palm for Hugo to slap it, but once again my son kept his hands behind his back.

"Come on Hugo, you're my mate..."

"No, you're not my friend," replied Hugo, turning his back to him.

"You're too protective of your son. You'll stop him from growing up," Idriss said to me, annoyed.

"Have you forgotten how you were with your own mother? You've forgotten who you are!"

I insisted that they took me to hospital. I had lost so much weight, and I thought they were finally starting to realise I was sick. They proposed taking me to the Islamic State hospital. I refused. There was no question of me setting foot in that place – I'd be more likely to pick up an infection in there and die than anything else. I wanted to go to a private clinic I'd heard people talking about. If I could make it there, I thought to myself, I could find a way of speaking with someone and asking for help. After a few days of thinking about it – during which I imagined the boys asked permission from a superior – they agreed. I was sure this would be my only chance and was utterly focussed on making a success of it. But there was no room for mistakes.

When we arrived at the waiting room, guarded closely by Mohammed with a gun slung over his shoulder, I was struck by the atmosphere in the clinic. Men and women came and went, working together and talking to each other without any awkwardness, even though the women's faces were uncovered. This perfectly natural scene, the same kind of atmosphere in which I'd grown up, now seemed exceptional. The fact that Daesh's highest officials tolerated this place was proof to me that they had no desire to let themselves be butchered in their own hospital either.

I felt like I could breathe again. But the presence of Mohammed, who followed me like my shadow, made sure I didn't relax. I stared hard at secretaries, doctors and nurses, in the hope they would see the cry for help in my eyes. But I imagine I was not the only woman in distress and perhaps they knew they could do nothing for me. I waited my turn, full of hope. When my name was called for the consultation, Mohammed got up to follow me. Before I had time to say anything, the doctor stopped him.

"Consultations take place in private."

"I'll stay by the door," said Mohammed. "That's the condition."

"Do you agree?" the doctor asked me.

I lowered my head. Ok, let's try, I thought. Perhaps I could whisper a few words to him.

He examined me behind a screen. I was painfully conscious of Mohammed's presence, a few meters away, holding Hugo by the hand. How could I explain to the doctor? He looked at me with such kindness. He'd help me if he could, I was certain of it.

He put his stethoscope back around his neck and began to walk away, scribbling down a prescription as he went. Then he was gone. Sapped of all energy, I pulled my clothes back on. I picked up the prescription at the welcome desk and paid for the consultation.

After that day, the boys let me return four times to the clinic, once on my own when I was able to call Julien. They did the operation on my ovarian cyst, but even then I was under such tight surveillance that I didn't have the chance to speak to anyone. Even so, I found some comfort in the familiar atmosphere of the clinic. It felt normal.

"You see how well we treat you Sophie?" the boys said to me, when they brought me back to the house after the operation.

One Sunday when they'd brought our food, I heard Idriss telling Hugo to put his shoes on. It was the time of the early evening prayer. I was in the kitchen and hurried to where they were standing.

"What did you say?"

"I was speaking to the kid."

"But what did you say to him? It looks like he's about to cry!"

Hugo looked upset and on the edge of tears.

"I'm taking him to the mosque. There's no place for unbelievers here."

"You're taking him nowhere – don't you dare touch my son!"

The slap fell hard across my face, and my head slammed against the wall from its force. Hugo screamed. I touched my burning face with my hand. I was filled with icy rage. I had no fear. I was nothing but a block of pure hatred. I walked towards Idriss.

"I know your mother, she used to cry in my arms after you left. But if she knew what you've become, she'd wish you dead as much as I do."

As Idriss lifted his hand again, Hugo threw himself between us and leapt up at Idriss, punching him with his tiny fists and crying. I fell to my knees to pull him back. I was afraid that Idriss might hit him. It was the moment I realised – at last – that the three men in front of me had nothing in common with the boys I once knew and was so fond of.

It was difficult to calm Hugo down that evening. He was crying for his father, which broke my heart. I was full of admiration at the courage and strength of my little boy. I felt dreadfully guilty and swore to myself I'd get him back to Paris, to Julien, whatever it took.

I didn't feel any fear. I knew the only alternative was death, so I had to succeed.

13: The *Madafa*

That same evening, the boys came back to the apartment after prayers. They rapped out their special knock and came inside, their faces closed and hard.

"Pack your bags. You're off to the *madafa* tomorrow."

The madafa was a kindergarten – for women. Some were there voluntarily, while others were locked up against their will. The mujaheddin left their wives there so someone could keep an eye on them while the men went away to fight. Women waiting to be allocated a husband were kept there, as were those who were uncooperative...The madafa was not exactly a prison; it was more like a kennel. Its location was a well-kept secret. I think the boys expected I'd cry and beg not to be sent there. They were wrong.

"I don't give a damn about your threats. You can take me wherever you want, so long as it's far from you!"

Idriss clenched his fists. He was shaking with anger.

"How ungrateful can you be? After everything we've done for you! You want to play the Westerner? They'll teach you a lesson at the madafa, you'll see."

I shrugged my shoulders. Anything rather than wither away inside these walls. But I needed something from them before they left.

"Give me my mobile," I demanded, speaking as though we were in the ghetto. There was nothing between us now except anger and hate.

Idriss didn't reply. I picked up a bottle.

"This is going in your face if you don't give me my phone back. I'm not going anywhere without it. You hear me?" I was shouting.

I think they thought they'd have to grab me by the hair and drag me out of there, kicking and screaming, through the streets. Without replying, Idriss pulled my phone from his pocket and waved it in my face. He must have thought it would be of no use to me in the madafa, because there was no network there and I didn't have any credit on it.

"Be ready at 8am tomorrow."

"Oh, I'll ready. I'll be waiting by the door!"

They left, carefully locking the door behind them. We were alone. I stored my mobile safely away with my family documents. I hid what money I had left in the lining of my bag, in the hope that they wouldn't search me too carefully when I was admitted to the madafa. I packed our bags, thinking back to the expectations I'd had when we arrived a couple of months ago. Although I felt weakened from not eating, I was clear-headed and alert, as though I'd woken up. The fog which had enveloped me since we arrived had melted away. I left the apartment in a mess on purpose, to humiliate the boys and give them some work to do. You take your revenge where you can.

I didn't sleep that night. I lay there trembling, holding Hugo in my arms, jumping at the slightest noise. I thought they might change their minds and want to keep my son. According to the law there, they were forbidden from taking him away from me because he was only four years old. But I was afraid of their stupidity, of their brutality. Their irrationality scared me, and my powerlessness was terrifying. They could have me killed under the pretext that I'd been leaking information to people in France, I imagined, or even just because I wanted to go home. Perhaps it was the Islamic State police who were coming for me the next day.

I started getting ready when I heard the first prayer at sunrise. I put on my niqab, then I woke up Hugo and gave him his breakfast. I dressed him in warm clothes and we sat in the hallway, where the boys found me at 8.15am. They seemed disappointed that I hadn't cried a single tear. I was stony-faced and not letting any emotion show through. The hatred I felt was such that it had taken the place of every other feeling. It gave me energy. The boys had become monsters and I wasn't going to let them ruin my son's life. It was freedom or death for us.

I lifted Hugo in my arms and they followed me with my suitcase. We stepped outside the building and they hailed a taxi. As we drove through the streets, I tried to get my bearings. It might come in useful, I thought. I recognised the Ferdous mosque, so we were in the centre of Raqqa. The boys suddenly told the taxi to stop. Idriss jumped out and went up to an Islamic State militia man. The two of them exchanged pleasantries, then the man approached the car. He greeted Mohammed, gave me a brief glance and then climbed into the car. He was a French jihadist, whose soft voice and gentle eyes gave him the air of an ardent believer. His bearing chilled me to the bone; it was clear the boys were in awe of him.

"Where have you been?" Idriss asked him. "I've been trying to get in touch with you."

"I was in Daraa," he replied, simply, without going into any more detail.

The boys' admiration was palpable as the car fell silent again. Daraa was a combat zone in the south of the country, not far from the border with Jordan. The Islamic State was sending small bands of fighters to attack the Free Syrian Army there, which itself was fighting against government forces. It was the city of Daraa which led the protest movement against Bashar in 2012.

The three boys ignored me and I returned the favour, my face turned towards the window. It was no longer blood that flowed through my veins, it was pure rage. The boys told the driver to stop the car well before we reached our destination – their distrust of the local people was such that they didn't want the driver to know the location of such a large number of women. We got out at one end of a busy street and set off on foot. As the three boys joked with each other, I walked along like a convict on death row: mechanically, one foot after the other, filled with dreams of revenge.

It was goodbye for me and the boys. I thought once again about everything I'd done for them, their sisters and their mothers. I was consumed by such hatred I could hardly breathe. The militiaman pointed out a building, then went back to the taxi as we walked up to the door. The building was like any other, with no sign to suggest otherwise. There was a locked metal grill in front of the door, and a camera looked down at us. The boys rang the bell, and then we waited: the residents would have to cover themselves, so as not to risk being seen. Finally, two women came and opened the door. Idriss spoke to them in Arabic, but they heard his accent and answered him in French.

"We've come to drop off this sister."

"For how long?"

"Oh, she'll be staying."

The door opened wider, and the boys dumped my luggage in the entrance then leaned over to hug Hugo, who ignored them. They said nothing to me, not even "goodbye". I stepped inside without looking back.

The two women introduced themselves. Umm Ferdouz was from France and the other was a young woman from Belgium, who told me eagerly that she was soon to be married. Not long after, the woman in charge of the madafa arrived. Umm Hakim was a heavy-set French woman of Moroccan heritage. Her face was round with barely any wrinkles, and it was difficult to guess her age but I thought she must be more than fifty. She was the oldest person there by far. Dressed in black from head to foot, a set of handcuffs hung from her waist, and she carried a pistol in her leather waistcoat. She took me to a room on the ground floor with a television and told me to wait for her, as she had things to do.

Images of a young Jordanian pilot being burned alive were playing on loop. Out of consideration for Hugo, whose eyes I'd covered, one of the other women there changed the channel and put on a children's programme – propaganda cartoons in Arabic. Hugo settled himself in front of the coffee table. Using gestures, another woman suggested that she show me around the place. Children started coming down the stairs. The madafa was overflowing with people. Women and children were locked up and living on top of each other. But Hugo was happy to see some other children at last and ran towards them. I lifted the veil from my eyes, but kept the rest of myself covered.

It was a long time before Umm Hakim returned from her office, out of breath and complaining theatrically about her lot.

"I'm all alone here and have to do everything! It's a nightmare. My son used to help me before, at least. He was in charge of exterior relations. But now I can't manage any more. It takes such a long time to get these marriages sorted! These girls have only one thing in their heads and that's to marry a fighter!"

She waddled along with the air of a kindly matron, full of enthusiasm. But I couldn't take my eyes off the pistol sticking out of her waistcoat, like a sausage. I stared at the women around me. How could I know who was a collaborator and who was a victim? I said nothing, not giving anything away, but walked behind Umm Hakim listening with one ear to her explanations. I tried hard to take everything in, to understand how the place was organised, so I could try to escape the moment I had the chance.

Umm Hakim had a set of keys hung around her neck. One of the inmates, a French woman, brought her another one which she added to her collection. This told me it that it was possible to gain her confidence. I forced myself to keep an friendly expression on my face and to hide my anxiety. I didn't know what the boys had said about me. If they hadn't told her I was a rebel, I might be able to get round her. I exchanged a few words with Umm Ferdouz, the French woman who'd opened the door earlier. In Islam, *firdous* means the highest level of paradise for Muslims...She told me that she came from the Paris region. We were the same age, both in our early 30s. Her eyes were glazed, as though she might be on medication. I sensed she was highly unstable. She seemed to be Umm Hakim's right-hand woman, whom she was visibly trying to impress. I decided to be careful around her. She asked me a few questions, and I was very careful not to give her any idea that I wanted to leave. The women running this place were loyal to Daesh.

Umm Hakim assigned Hugo and me a room on the first floor. It was about 10 metres square, with toilets and a shower cubicle inside, like a cell. The level of cleanliness left much to be desired, so I asked for a broom. Old habits die hard; even if I was planning to run away the next day, I couldn't bear the thought of my son sleeping in such a filthy place. The French woman brought me a clean bedcover, a sponge and some cleaning products, and I set myself to work. Scrubbing the floor calmed me down; the familiar, mechanical task allowed me to think of other things. I could almost be back at home, doing the housework. I could be anywhere.

Umm Firdouz, still looking out of it, explained how the madafa functioned. Once a week, each woman received a basket of food containing fruit, fresh almonds, nuts, beans, pasta, honey cakes, powdered milk, and tins of sardine and tuna. There was a supplement for each child. Everyone cooked their own meals and kept their food in their room. The provisions were generous, she told me with pride, as though life there was a veritable bed of roses.

Once the room was clean, I went to have a look round the premises. The other women I met greeted me, and each time I tried to work out if they were a prisoner like me. Who might be on my side? The only other black woman, an Australian Somali, offered me some pasta for Hugo. Laughing, she said she didn't know how to cook for one, and she'd made too much as usual. I accepted, and the three of us sat in her room. She was very young. Pregnant and divorced, she was waiting for her baby to be born and perhaps to remarry. We spoke in English. Like all the single women in the building, she shared her room with a young Syrian woman married to a foreigner, who soon joined us. Smiling, but very shy, she seemed extremely proud of her jihadist husband, who'd left her in the madafa while he went off to fight.

She played with Hugo, calling him "my little husband". But Hugo was not impressed. "I don't want to," he said, then whispered to me, "it's you I want to marry." That made us all laugh and for a moment we were just three women having fun together, despite our different situations. Then the feeling passed. I felt for these women but I knew I was completely alone, with my own battle to fight.

Two more young girls joined us. I thought one of them must be a minor – I wouldn't have given her more than 17 years. She'd known her husband in Australia, but hinted that he'd changed after they arrived in Raqqa. She didn't go as far as saying she wanted to go home, but she seemed terribly sad. Her friend had got married without ever having met the man, who was represented by a brother. She too seemed to be proud of being chosen.

I asked them questions about the organisation of the madafa and Umm Hakim's schedule, but was scared of arousing their suspicions. When Hugo finished eating, we went back downstairs to the ground floor, accompanied by the young Australian. In the TV room, there were now images of a beheading playing out on the screen. I recognised Nicolas, the French convert the boys had pointed out to me with such admiration when we'd gone to the market during my first few days in Raqqa. My heart turned over. They were monsters. The Australian woman covered her eyes, saying that she didn't want to see violent images for fear they would traumatise her unborn child. But the others laughed as the beheadings took place. I turned my head and looked through the window, which opened onto a small yard. I wondered whether I could climb up from there. Above it, I could see a barbed wire fence, which seemed to border a roof or terrace. Realising one of the women was staring at me, I forced myself to look at the unbearable scenes on the television playing out one after another.

A bit later, I walked slowly around the madafa, continuing my inspection. Right at the end of a corridor on the first floor, there was a glass door that opened onto a terrace – the same one I'd seen from downstairs. The door was locked, but I could see that the terrace adjoined the neighbouring building. If I climbed up the small wall from the courtyard on the ground floor, perhaps I could hoist myself up there. Then we could just drop down the other side onto the street. But would Hugo hurt himself jumping from such a height?

That evening, while I made Hugo his dinner with the food the others had shared with me, there was a discussion going on about how one woman wanted to leave her husband, and how he wouldn't let her. According to Islam, a woman could request a divorce on the grounds that her conjugal needs were repeatedly not being met. I pricked my up ears as I tried to work out whether she wanted to go back to her country, listening out for the slightest clue. If I could find another woman like me, we could try to escape together. As I fed Hugo, I told myself I needed to start eating again to build up my strength, but I couldn't do it. I felt as though I could no longer swallow, that the smallest mouthful would stick in my throat.

From the living room, the windows looked out onto the street. They were made from tinted glass, so that no one on the street could see inside. But from our side, we could see the street and the people walking around. A group of very young women watched excitedly as a band of mujaheddin walked past. They were acting like schoolgirls on a day trip. I couldn't understand how they could be so light-hearted.

Suddenly, I noticed two women standing apart from the others in a corner of the room. One was the young Syrian

woman who'd seemed so sad, the other was one of the
women who'd said she was divorced. One of them hid something in the folds of her abaya and my heart leapt.

It was a telephone.

Later on, I managed to find one of them on her own. We
chatted for a bit, and she told me she had four children.
She'd been abandoned by her husband, so she was here
waiting to see if anyone else could be found for her. I came
clean and told her I'd seen the phone. She lowered her voice
and told me she had some credits, and that she'd been able
to get a wifi signal – it was weak, but enough to send a single
message. She was hesitant and I felt she didn't trust me, but
finally she promised to bring the phone to my room that
evening.

I waited for her a long time after I tucked Hugo up in bed.
In vain. She hadn't dared.

It was a difficult night.

The next day, I rose early and made Hugo his breakfast.
Then I went down to ask Umm Hakim if I could go to the
clinic. I explained that I needed follow-care after the operation I'd had. Umm Hakim was sympathetic and said she'd
take me to the public hospital. Without openly criticising
the hospital managed by Daesh, I reasoned that it would
be better for me to return to the clinic where I'd been
treated and to see the same doctor. Umm Hakim wasn't
keen, but in the end she agreed. I wanted to ask the doctor
to contact Julien for me. I knew that the Syrians who worked
there weren't under the command of Daesh. Would he dare
help me? I didn't know, but I couldn't think of anything else
I could do.

I knew there was no chance Umm Hakim would allow me
to go alone, but I hoped she'd send one of the other women
with me – preferably Umm Ferdouz. I'd have no trouble giving her the slip. At that moment, Umm Ferdouz appeared
carrying Umm Hakim's breakfast on a tray, along with her
various medications. Umm Hakim was not in good health.

She'd never catch me if I made a run for it. As weak as I was
from my hunger strike, I was sure to be faster than her.

I went back to the dormitory to get ready. I dressed Hugo
in warm clothes. It was a cold morning, but more impor-
tantly, I thought we might be outside for a long time. If we
had to hide somewhere or spend the night outside, we'd
need to be well wrapped up. I also took Hugo's laptop, so
I could hide some things in the pocket: underwear, spare
socks, some biscuits and cakes, just in case. All the time, the
same words kept going around my head like a refrain: *we
must escape today*. It was a fight for our survival. When
I went downstairs, Umm Hakim chided me for being too
clingy with Hugo. He'd never grow up to be a good fighter if
I mollycoddled him like that, she told me. I smiled and
agreed, but pointed out that I was just trying to protect him
as best as I could, given we were in a foreign country, and his
father wasn't with us. I tried to give the appearance of being
docile.

As we were about to leave I realised both Umm Hakim
and Umm Ferdouz were coming with me. The disappointment was crushing. We went downstairs and Umm Ferdouz
opened the internal door into the lobby. I walked through it.
Then she opened the front door. At that moment, a voice
rang out from inside the building. The two women told me
to wait for them.

"Get in the car," Umm Hakim said.

Hugo and I were alone at the door, looking out onto the
street. The sunlight flooded in, golden and blindingly
bright. I froze for several terrifying moments. It was a chance
and perhaps the only one I'd have. But if they came back
down now, Hugo and I would only be a few seconds in front
of them. They'd catch us, beat us and lock us up for good,
and all hope of escape would be gone. I took a step into the
light, gripping my son's little hand with all my strength.
I could hear nothing but the sound of blood pounding in
my ears.

"Why aren't you in the car?"

The two women were back. Umm Hakim scrutinised my face. I pulled the veil down over my eyes.

"I was waiting for you," I replied quietly.

A cloud drifted across the sun.

Women weren't allowed to drive in Raqqa, but Umm Hakim sat down behind the wheel and drove off confidently into the traffic. This helped me understand her position in Daesh's hierarchy. Sitting in the back seat with Hugo, I tried once more to work out where I was in the city. We drove to the clinic and went inside. Once again, I felt relief at being in this place where women went about their business alongside their male colleagues, their faces uncovered. I walked up to the reception desk and asked if I could see the same doctor who examined me the first time – the one who'd protested when Mohammed followed us into the consultation room.

"I'm sorry, he's in Aleppo with his family," the secretary told us. "But any of the other doctors here can see you."

"She can't be seen by a man," Umm Hakim cut in.

"But there are only male doctors here, my sister," I said.

"Well, one of them can look at you, but not touch you."

"But what about the examination?"

"Impossible. It's forbidden."

Her enormous chin was wobbling with indignation. I backed down. Not long after, a doctor came to find me. I got up and gave Hugo to the two women, but Umm Hakim stood up too.

"I'm coming."

"Stay with the boy, Umm Hakim."

"No, there has to be a woman present. Then I can help with the translation, too."

She followed us into the examination room. I was beaten. It wouldn't work.

The doctor could see I wasn't well. I was thin and very lethargic. I knew my hunger strike had led to nothing, but even so I found it impossible to start eating again. I felt half dead. He insisted on taking blood and urine tests. This time

Umm Ferdouz came with me for the urine test. The result was immediate. I had cystitis and was running a fever. The doctor prescribed antibiotics.

"Are you eating properly?" the doctor asked me. "You need to eat plenty of fruit and vegetables,' he advised me, gently. I knew I needed to get my strength back if I wanted to escape.

Back at the reception area, Umm Hakim paid for my consultation and tests. While we were provided for in the madafa, she was furious at having to pay medical costs when a visit to the Daesh hospital would have been free. She took out her bad temper on the secretaries, recommending – in a manner both authoritarian and semi-maternal – that they should cover themselves better. The young women nodded and readjusted their headscarves. They were afraid. What reply could they give to a woman with a gun poking out from under her arm?

Umm Hakim interrogated me in the car on the way back.

"I haven't see you pray today."

I lied, saying I had my period. Then she and Umm Ferdouz told me the story of a French woman who'd come to the madafa the year before.

"It was a bizarre case. She arrived all alone, without knowing anyone in Raqqa. We took her into the madafa with us. As you know, I knock on all the doors in the morning to wake everyone up for the first prayer, and I noticed she wasn't praying. She *never* prayed. A bit suspect, don't you think?

"So Umm Hakim made an inspection," Umm Ferdouz chipped in, breathlessly. "She searched the girl's room. And you know what she found?"

I didn't reply.

"We found the visiting card of one of Bashar's officials." Umm Hakim's voice was grave. I looked at her face in the wing mirror – she'd lifted her veil while she was driving. Was this a threat? Her face was impassive.

"What happened to the girl?"

"I don't know. She ran away. We never heard of her again."

At that, the two women seemed to lose interest in the story and moved onto something else. Suddenly, I wondered if they'd set a trap for me that morning by leaving me alone next to the open front door. Perhaps they were testing me. Once again, I had a strong sense that Umm Hakim didn't trust me. I wasn't going to survive long in the madafa.

When we got back, we ate our lunch together with the rest of the women. My neighbour took a swig from a bottle of water, then kindly handed it to me. I put it down without touching it. This didn't escape Umm Hakim, who was watching me carefully.

"You behave like a Westerner."

"I can't help that – it's how I was brought up."

"Well, you're going to have to change. It's not acceptable. When I was in Afghanistan, I used to drink from ponds!"

She spoke as though she'd been in many war zones. That might have been the case; something told me that behind her the sanctimonious grandmother act, Umm Hakim was as tough as leather.

"Umm Hakim has been in prison in France and in Afghanistan," Umm Ferdouz whispered admiringly to me.

In the madafa, the girls only thought and talked about one thing: marriage. It was a big deal. They talked about their husbands. They wished for a husband. They wanted to change their husbands. The entire lives of these woman, shut up within these four walls, revolved around men who roamed freely around the city. The best, apparently, was a young *mujahid*. They talked about men in the coarsest way, comparing their preferences for white ones, black ones, Westerners and Arabs, and imparting to each other their expert advice.

There was a lot of excitement that day because Umm Hakim was receiving a *mujahid* who was coming, with two brothers as witnesses, to ask for the hand of a young Belgian woman who was there with her mother and sisters. The young bride to be was so happy and her mother was bursting

with pride. There was a party-like atmosphere. Only the
Australian, with her huge stomach, looked on with some
reserve, melancholic and silent.

All the women were busy preparing for the important
visit. We scrubbed the corridors and plumped up the cushions in the meeting room, the small living room and in
Umm Hakim's office. The young Belgian woman was
glowing.

"Are you happy?" I asked.

"Are you kidding me? I'm going to be with a man!"

It was hard not to laugh, despite myself.

"You might not find it as extraordinary as you think..."

But she wasn't going to let me dampen her enthusiasm,
and the other women were encouraging her. Between them,
they talked about sex in a very crude manner.

I asked Umm Hakim if I could go to the market. She bat-
ted me away with her hand, as if I was a fly. I asked again,
gently, as persistent as a child.

"Wait...and I'll see," she said finally, just to get rid of me.

But I took her words literally and went to get my handbag.
I waited patiently at the entrance, in front of the door to the
lobby. There was always constant coming and going at the
madafa. Several times the door was left open, but there were
always women in the corridor. I asked again if I could go out.

"In an hour," Umm Hakim told me, exasperated when
I insisted that she should take me.

I went back up to the dormitory and took Hugo to the
toilet. Then I dressed him in another layer of clothes – jeans
on top of his tracksuit bottoms and a second t-shirt. He
looked like a little Michelin Man. I did the same for myself.
I didn't take the computer this time, but I stuffed my handbag with everything I could. Then we went downstairs and
waited in front of the door. Perhaps there would be a chance,
I thought to myself. I mustn't miss it if it comes.

"Get out of the way, the men are coming!"

Everyone fled to the TV room, the women crowding
around the cracks in the door to catch a glimpse of the men,

who'd entered the building. There were two or three of them, one of whom was a rugged mixed race man, provoking longing sighs all around me. Umm Hakim fussed around them, bringing them into her office where the mother of the young woman waited to receive them. The bride was standing to one side of me, trembling and waiting to be called. There was no one behind them to lock the doors as they came in. The marriage had been arranged by Umm Hakim and the bride had never seen her husband-to-be, but she hoped that it was the mixed race one, she whispered in my ear. She'd heard a lot of good things about those guys. She was only a child, naïve and ignorant. I didn't know what to say to her, so I just smiled. She'd already refused one offer. Refusing a marriage proposal was the only freedom women had. Today she was going to exercise her free will for the last time. If only I could take her under my wing and hide her there...But there was nothing I could do. I felt as though I was watching a lamb going to the slaughter. She bombarded me with questions – how is the wedding night? Her mother had told her that her *mujahid* would treat her like a princess. I said nothing.

"Umm Ferdouz, please come." Umm Hakim's voice called out.

Umm Ferdouz was shaking. She covered herself and the young bride, then both of them left the room. I saw them walk up to Umm Hakim's office. Umm Ferdouz didn't go inside. Umm Hakim said something to her, and she went out into the street. In the TV room, the women were chattering excitedly.

I took Hugo by the hand and left the room. The door of Umm Hakim's office was shut. There was no one in the corridor. I pushed the door of the lobby and it opened without a sound. I saw the sunlight streaming through the open front door. Outside, to the right of the doorway, Umm Ferdouz was deep in conversation with a man – probably her husband. She had her back to me.

I knew that this was the moment. I moved forward as though a hand was pushing me from behind. There was no time to be afraid, to doubt, or to hesitate. It was now or never. Hugo stared up at me, questioningly.

"We're going to buy something to eat," I said to him. If we were caught, I didn't want him to give us away.

Holding him firmly by the hand, I slipped out into the street. The sun sparkled. Umm Ferdouz didn't look round. I walked swiftly in the opposite direction towards freedom.

We walked, without rushing, as far as the corner of the lane on which the madafa was situated. I didn't let myself look back and held my head high, as though I had every right to be there. All the time, I was expecting to hear Umm Ferdouz calling after me, or to be suddenly grabbed by the collar. But nothing happened. I turned the corner. I could no longer be seen from the madafa.

It was a busy street, with heavy traffic. I began breathing faster. We were on the run. I caught sight of a group men in front of us, bearded Daesh guys. I kept walking. Suddenly, Hugo tripped over.

"Be careful!" I hissed.

My son looked up at me in surprise, then climbed to his feet. We walked past the men, who didn't say anything to us. I turned into the next street and gathered Hugo up into my arms. We were wandering deeper into a maze of small streets and alleys. I was trying to put as much distance as possible between us and the madafa. But my hunger strike had left me very weak, and I couldn't carry Hugo any longer. I put him down and crouched in front of him.

"We're going to play a game now, Hugo. We're going to run. You have to run like the wind, as fast as Flash McQueen. Are you ready to do that?"

"Oh yes, mama. I'm going to run as fast as I can!"

Flash McQueen, a car in the animated film "Cars", was my son's hero. Hugo launched himself forwards on the pavement with all the strength he had in his little legs. He charged off so fast that I had a job keeping up with him, caught up in the folds of my burqa and hardly able to see through my veil. We ran for our lives through the streets of Raqqa, running towards our freedom. And Hugo could run. *Keep going, my love*, I thought as I watched his little legs whirring. As he ran, he looked back at me.

"Keep going, mama, you'll make it too. Run, mama, run!"

I spurred myself on. It was my son who was carrying *me* now and giving me courage. We came out onto a bigger road, and I started looking around for a taxi. I approached the first one whose driver had a friendly face – a clean-shaven, grandfatherly Syrian.

"Where's your *mahram*?" he asked. "Who's your guardian?"

I repeated the name of the clinic, but he shook his head. He wasn't going to risk taking a woman on her own. He stared straight ahead, and I moved off quickly. After three or four attempts, just as I was starting to get desperate, one of them agreed to take us.

The doctor *had* to be back from Aleppo. I was going to ask him to get in touch with my family. I'd confess we'd run away and beg for his help. Surely he couldn't refuse to help us.

We arrived. I went inside the clinic and spoke with one of the secretaries that Umm Hakim had been lecturing earlier that morning. I asked to see a doctor. The young woman replied that all the doctors had left, and that I'd have to come back the next day. I pulled my veil up, showing her my panic-stricken face. Despite my efforts, tears were rolling down my face. The words spilled out so fast I could hardly breath.

"I beg you, I've got nowhere else to go, you have to help me, *please*!" I stuttered in English.

She smiled at me. Her expression was as impenetrable as that of the first taxi driver who'd refused to take us.

"You'll need to come back tomorrow," she said.

"Please, let me spend the night here!"

"I'm sorry, there are no beds available."

I felt as though my head was going to explode. I lowered my voice.

"Could I stay with you, at your home? Just one night? I'm begging you..."

I saw the naked fear flickering in her eyes as I spoke. Her smile didn't falter, but I knew she was thinking of Umm Hakim and her revolver. She wasn't going to help me. Why should she risk her life for someone she didn't even know? I pleaded with her again, but I knew I was wasting my time. I'd managed to escape, but I was still caught like a rat in a trap in this town where I knew no one. The niqab meant I couldn't be recognised in the street, but also made me a target. No one would help me. The entire city was living under a reign of terror. We were lost.

We left the clinic. My legs were shaking, and I couldn't think of what to do. We wandered aimlessly through the streets. It would be evening soon and we needed to find a place to hide. I'd be able to think more clearly tomorrow. I thought of one of the big building sites I'd noticed on the first day we'd arrived in Raqqa. But at night the temperature dropped dramatically. I was worried Hugo would freeze despite the thick clothes I'd wrapped him in.

The Syrian woman from the block of flats where I'd stayed came into my mind. She was the only person who'd been friendly with me since I came to Raqqa. It hadn't been much, it was true – just a question and the smile I heard in her voice. Nothing more. But I didn't have anyone else, or any other ideas.

I decided I'd go and knock at her door. In the same building where we'd been living. The same building where the boys were. I was putting myself into the lion's den, but it was my only hope.

There were several taxis parked in the street, waiting for customers. I walked slowly past them, trying work out which one might agree to take us. I was terrified of being denounced.

Not him – he was wearing Afghan-style clothes, a sign that he'd aligned himself with Daesh. Not that one, either – his beard was too well trimmed. The third one had short hair, a smooth forehead and was clean shaven. I approached him hopefully and asked if he could drop us at the central market. In my panic and exhaustion I couldn't remember the name of the Daesh hospital, which was the closest landmark to the apartment building. But I could find my way to the flats from the market. After a slight hesitation and a quick look around us, he let us into his car. We were soon stuck in traffic, and I tried to read his face in the wing mirror. He wasn't playing *nasheed* on the radio – the victory chants, that were the only form of music allowed by the Islamic State. Suddenly, I took a chance and asked him if he could drive us to the border. He didn't speak English, but the fear made me creative. I told him I was a *muhajir* – a foreigner.

"Sanliurfa," I said.

It was the name of the Turkish village on the border that I'd passed through. I managed to come up with the Arabic words for "family" and "money".

"I'll pay, I'll pay," I repeated, pointing to my bag.

The man listened. Then he pulled over and signalled to me to wait in the car. I watched him get out of the car. He walked towards a small shop selling combat clothing. I didn't let him out of my sight, my nerves on edge. In front of the shop, the shopkeeper and another man were talking. He was a Western convert. This was not good, not good at all. My driver was waiting respectfully for them to finish their conversation.

Without a second thought, I opened the door, grabbed Hugo by the hand and jumped out of the car into the oncoming traffic. I swept my son up into my arms and ran between the cars. I managed to get across the road and fled down the first side street, with Hugo clinging to me. His hands gripped each other behind my neck and his legs were around my waist, as I sprinted until I was out of breath. I could feel the stares from the men on street. Hugo's grip had flattened my robes against me and the outline of my body was visible. But I didn't stop.

I was hot and gasping for breath. The muscles in my arms were on fire. But I didn't let go of my son. I slowed down a bit, to attract less attention. I was trying to make my way to the building we'd lived in, but I didn't recognise any of the streets. We walked for an hour, this way and that, before I began to recognise where we were.

15: In the Lion's Den

At the bottom of the large spiral staircase in the apartment block there was a kind of box room, which was used to store cleaning products, furniture and empty flower pots. It was impossible to be sure we wouldn't bump into anyone, but I had no choice – we couldn't stay for long on the street. Still holding Hugo in my arms, I entered the building. The hall was empty. I headed straight for the room and dived inside, closing the door behind us. Finally.

I was completely exhausted. I let myself slide down onto the floor. Hugo huddled against me, and I slowly got my breath back in the darkness.

"Hugo, you mustn't make a sound. We're going home to see papa. But for that to happen, you have to be very quiet. Do you understand? There are some bad uncles outside who don't want us to go back to papa. So we can't talk. Ok?"

My little boy nodded his head and kept his lips clamped shut. He didn't make a sound. I listened out for noise from the staircase. A man's footsteps echoed on the stairs above our heads, then grew fainter. I'd decided to wait until prayer time, as there'd be no risk of seeing anyone then. It was unthinkable for men to not to go for prayers. The shops had to pull their shutters down, and there were special patrols to make sure this rule was respected. In theory, latecomers to the mosque were to be caned. But more often, the punishment consisted of a few lashes, a fine and mandatory attendance of an indoctrination session. It wasn't good to be considered a rulebreaker Daesh's regime. For the women, things were a bit more flexible due to the rule that excused us from prayers during our periods.

Finally, I heard the call to prayer resounding through the city. I waited a few more moments to be sure everyone had gone to the mosque then I took Hugo's hand, and we crept out of the box room. As we climbed the stairs, I could barely lift my feet – it felt as though I'd spent all my energy on that final, frantic dash through the streets of Raqqa. I was painfully conscious of the fact that this was my last chance. If the woman closed the door in my face, we'd be left to wander the streets until we were captured. Then we'd be separated. That would mean death for me and for Hugo, an orphanage, Quranic school and such loneliness, such distress that it terrified me to think of it.

At the fourth floor, I spotted some sandals outside the door. There were no men's shoes – the father would be at the mosque for the prayer. I knocked.

After a short time, the door opened. The Syrian woman had only a scarf draped around her hair. Her simple, honest face looked worried already. A knock at the door always carried the risk of bad news. I pulled back my veil. Tears flowed down my face, just as they had done earlier in front of the secretary at the clinic. I didn't say a word. I stared at her, my face wet.

She looked at me, her eyes widening with fear as she took in the situation. I could see she was about to close the door. Then she caught sight of Hugo, standing at my side in silence, just as I'd told him. Her face twitched and she stepped backwards, gesturing at me to come inside.

We took off our shoes, and she led us into the living room. Madana spoke English. I told her my story. She was stunned. How had I ended up here in such a mess, when I wasn't even from Syria? She'd have fled the war if she could. And why didn't I go back to France, which I could do as I was French? She found it hard to understand that this was prohibited by Daesh, and why I'd been held there against my will. But there again, anything was possible with those fools, she said.

"They're monsters. Murderers. They came here to torture our people."

She told me that a few months before I arrived, in a neighbouring square, dozens of men had been executed in public by foreign fighters. There had been stonings. As she spoke, she served us with cake and tea. I ate a little as I knew I had to get my strength back at all costs, but my stomach seemed to have shrunk. After just a few mouthfuls, I was full and felt almost nauseous. By contrast, Hugo ate with gusto as Madana kissed and cuddled him, sitting him on her lap. I didn't stop her. If she liked Hugo, she'd do anything to save him. Her own children also surrounded him, bringing their toys into the living room, but we made sure they didn't make too much noise.

"Do you know anyone who's left Syria?" I asked her.

"I don't know anyone who's even managed to get out of Raqqa. You've seen all the checkpoints outside the city? You need special permission to get past them."

At the end of the prayer, her husband came back home. She went into the hallway to welcome him and I heard them whispering to each other. Our lives were at stake. He came into the living room and greeted me. He was a small, round man and I could sense his fear as well. I felt ashamed for putting them in such danger, and begged his forgiveness. He nodded his head and explained that he was going to stay at a friend's place that evening. If the police came, they couldn't search the apartment if there was no man there. They'd have to bring a female policewoman, and there weren't many of them. That would give us some time. I thanked him, with my hands on my heart. Then he was gone, his generosity to me putting his wife and children in danger.

Madana and I started talking again.

"You can stay here for one night, but no longer. It's very dangerous. The place is full of Daesh men, as you know. The building and the neighbourhood are full of them. We can't keep you here."

"Thank you with all my heart. There must be a solution. Perhaps it's possible to find a smuggler?"

"I have no idea how," she said, sadly. "Who could we trust? It seems like it's easier in Tal Abiad."

She unfolded a map.

"Look, you could get there by bus. Then you could ask around..."

"But who to?"

"You'll see them at the bus station, the smugglers. It's close to the border."

"But how can I get out of Raqqa? I don't have the right to travel alone."

She shook her head despondently. She didn't know. There were no answers.

"Would it be possible to phone my husband?" I asked.

Madana called her older son, Hassani, and sent him to the cybercafé to buy some credits. He came back 20 minutes later. I tapped the code into the phone, then Julien's number, praying he'd answer.

"Pick up...please, pick up..."

He answered on the second ring, his voice trembling with emotion.

"Sophie?"

"Julien, we've escaped. Someone has to help me. You need to alert the DGSI."

"Julien, we're on the run. Someone has to help me. You need to tell the DGSI."

Sophie spoke fast.

"We got away from them. We're still in Raqqa, with a Syrian family, but I don't know if we can stay here for long. The family are very scared. They've told me we can only stay for 24 hours."

I'd gone to a buy a pizza that evening, when the phone rang. I froze. It was the ringtone I'd assigned to her number, a track we both loved. Its chorus, "There she comes" suddenly seemed especially apt. My wife and my son had been gone for two months, and I had hadn't heard any news from them for two weeks. Two weeks during which I spent every moment terrified of learning they were dead. Breathing fast, I stopped abruptly at the bottom of our apartment building in the darkness, the pizza cooling under my arm in a cardboard box, the phone clamped to my ear. Inform the DGSI? What did she think I'd been doing over the past few weeks?

When Sophie came back from her holiday in Senegal, where she'd stayed with the aunt of a boy from the community centre, and announced she was going away again, this time to Turkey, I was pleased she'd decided to take Hugo with her. I'd had enough of managing everything on my own. She'd been distant for several months, always preoccupied with her work, always focused on other people. Let her go, I'd thought. It will give us some space. There was something that didn't quite add up about her plans. But I was tired. I didn't probe.

The day before she left, I received an anonymous email signed "Jimmy Hendricks." It was typed in capitals and full of spelling mistakes. It seemed like a bad joke – but the words were unambiguous: *Your wife and your son are leaving for jihad. Watch out, you'll never see them again.*

I spent all day wondering about it. My older daughters from my previous marriage were at the house for the afternoon. I waited until after I'd dropped them back at their mother's, then called my wife.

"So it seems you're not planning to come back?"

I took in her stunned silence, then decided to push a bit.

"I'm outside the police station, Sophie, and I'm warning you – I'm going to inside to tell them."

I didn't believe it, though. Not really.

A torrent of words burst into my earpiece. Sophie was mad with rage, and she gave me an absolute tongue lashing. She was shocked that I'd even contemplate such nonsense. Leave for *jihad* with Hugo? Seriously? She told me that one of the young guys, who'd been excluded from the community centre for bad behaviour, must be playing tricks to get his own back. Her colleague Eric, one of my old schoolfriends, had received a threatening email too. Obviously, it wasn't to be taken seriously. It was the idiotic behaviour of an angry kid.

It didn't occur to me that attack is the best method of defence and that my wife's fury was a sign of her guilt. I believed her. I even asked her forgiveness for being ready to believe such an absurd idea. She told me she was going to sort it out, that she was going to call the young person she suspected of sending the email. I told her I'd see her later.

It was a Friday morning when I drove my wife and son to the airport, both of us sad and tired. I promised to keep the house clean. To make her laugh I sent her some pictures of me doing the housework just after I got home. I rearranged the furniture and changed the whole living room around. I knew we needed a break from each other, but I wanted it to work. I thought about us and our relationship all weekend. During this time, she was on her way to Syria.

On Monday afternoon, my mobile rang at the end of one of my classes. It was Eric, Sophie's colleague, and my old friend from high school. I picked up.

"Hi Julien. I was calling to ask about Sophie."

My pulse quickened. Why would he call me on my mobile to ask about my wife, his colleague?

"She's gone on holiday. In Turkey."

"Shit!"

I heard him speaking with someone.

"What? What's the matter? Eric?"

"Are you at home? I'll come over, with Fela."

We all arrived at my house at the same time. I sat them down in the living room. I was desperate to hear what they had to say, but was also scared. With good reason. They told me that Sophie had resigned a month before. The Tuesday before had been her last day and she'd refused to have a farewell drinks party.

"She'd changed." Both of them had known her since she started working at the community centre.

I sat listening to them.

"She really changed. She'd withdrawn into herself. She wouldn't talk to us anymore. She did some...bizarre things. She became close with certain families – Idriss' family especially. She went there every evening after work. We didn't know if you knew and didn't want to interfere..."

The information hit me in the face, like a swift succession of slaps. I tried to keep it together, as I struggled with my humiliation, fear and anger. All the lies from the past few months were now coming to light. The biggest one was her resignation. I looked at them, hardly daring to admit to myself what I was thinking. We all knew that Turkey the jumping off point for Syria – but I couldn't let myself think it. It was too much. Too insane.

"She'd never put Hugo in danger. She's a good mother."

"She was no longer friendly with me," said Fela quietly.

"It's impossible." I couldn't believe it.

Yet it was true that I didn't know where they were. The last text was sent the day before. I'd tried calling several times, but the mobile was switched off. Eric suggested talking to Idriss' brother. I agreed, and he agreed to meet us near his house. The three of us went to meet him.

Marwan was Idriss' older brother. The two had never been close. Marwan had always laughed at his younger brother for reverting to Islam, irritated by his moralising and inflexibility. When the youngest of their brothers became radicalised too, the relationship was strained to breaking point. Marwan had never forgiven Idriss for what he'd done to the family. Not only were their parents completely devastated, but one of the younger sisters had tried to follow in his footsteps and was currently in prison in Turkey with her boyfriend.

We sat in a café in the housing estate. Marwan immediately confessed he was the author of the message I'd received the day before Sophie left. I was furious.

"But why didn't you sign it? Why didn't you call me?"

"I don't know. I wasn't entirely sure myself. I was only guessing, but it was just that I'd seen your wife change. She was on Viber all the time with my bro. What he was saying must have gone to her head."

It was true that Sophie had been on her phone all the time lately. It was constantly vibrating. She was seldom at home, but even when she was around her head was somewhere else. Now I knew where.

"You know, that's what they want – the ones who leave. To bring others. Not to stay there alone like idiots."

"And do you really believe Sophie's in Syria?"

"I can't be sure of it, but I think so. Or at least she's on the way there now. I'm sorry, man. My brother's gone crazy, and he's left a trail of destruction behind him."

I went back home, alone. I felt like a robot. First of all, I tried calling the government hotline concerned with jihadist radicalisation, but the helpdesk closed at 5pm. It was too late. I searched on the internet and found the government website, www.stop- djihadisme.gouv.fr. I watched a video on the site, which was pretty basic and not very convincing, then looked at a document that resembled an aircraft safety card, to see if I could recognise my wife in what it said.

The warning signs were as follows: "Is she avoiding her old friends, now considering them as impure?" Sophie had never used such vocabulary in front of me. But it was true that she'd been going out less. She had her own friends, and I was learning that I'd been unaware of what she was doing. "Has she rejected members of her family?" Here I had to admit to myself that she'd been seeing much less of them than before. But that hadn't worried me – instead I had the impression that Sophie was finally becoming more independent, so I didn't make a fuss about it. But perhaps there had been other reasons. "Has she changed her eating habits?" It was true she no longer ate pork, but she carried on buying and cooking it for Hugo. She'd become a Muslim, I knew that, and she was trying to find her own way of practicing it. But it didn't seem to me that she was behaving like a fanatic. I continued reading.

"Has your family member dropped out of school or training?" Tick. She'd resigned in secret. My anxiety went up a notch. I ran through the rest of the questions quickly. Sophie hadn't stopped listening to music, but she had stopped doing Zumba classes and teaching them. An argument she told me she'd had with Idriss a few months ago came back to me. Idriss was up in arms about the women who wiggled their butts in the dance hall at the community centre. He'd wanted to forbid his sister from going there. The story hadn't bothered me at the time – these young guys who tried to control their sisters were nothing new; they were everywhere in the estates. Now I thought again, incredulous. If she really was going to Syria to join Daesh, then her beliefs had must have radically changed in barely a few months. It seemed completely unthinkable to me.

The next set of warning signs asked about how the person dressed, (this had changed a bit), political opinions (she never said anything) and whether the person visited Islamist propaganda sites on the internet. Of course this would have raised a flag, but I had no idea about the sites she looked at.

Out of nine of the "symptoms" listed, I considered she'd displayed three and a half. I crossed my fingers. Perhaps this wasn't the explanation. Perhaps I was imagining it all. I tried calling her mobile again, but when it went to voicemail again, I decided to click on the icon on the website which said: "Do you wish to report a situation of concern?" I filled in a form, gave our address and wrote a summary of my worries. In the box where it asked, "How is the person related to you?" I clicked on "other", because the only choices were "mother/father" or "sister/brother". I stated that I wished to be contacted. I never heard from them.

I put my jacket back on and went to the police station.

"I've come to report a missing person. It's my wife."

The policeman on duty exchanged an ironic glance with his colleague.

"Your wife has disappeared?"

"Yes, with our four-year-old son."

At this, he straightened up and seemed ready to take things rather more seriously. It was two o'clock in the morning. I gave him a summary of what had happened. When he heard that Sophie had been born in Cameroon, the cops exchanged another look which seemed to say, "Well, there you go – he should have chosen his wife more carefully." I told myself not to get upset; I wasn't going to reform the national police service that night.

They asked me a series of tick-box questions, which they painstakingly read from a grid. Many of the questions were the same as the ones on the website. I replied with care, trying not to hide anything or to exaggerate. I still wasn't certain whether I was just imagining things. But when I said that my wife had emptied the savings account of our son to finance their trip to Turkey, the policeman raised an eyebrow.

"How much was it?"

"There was 1,300 euros in there."

He looked appalled at my stupidity. How could I explain to them how things had been going with her? That this "humanitarian trip" had seemed like a solution – both for the discontent she'd wrestled with for so long and for our relationship, which was on the brink of falling apart?

I let it go. I left at 5am and went home to sleep. The police called several hours later. The two from the night shift had passed on my information, and their colleagues wanted me to come back that morning. I went immediately and was questioned again. They knew Idriss, Mohammed and Souleymane, and this time the questions seemed more relevant and more targeted than the night before. They were accompanied by a man who told introduced himself as an officer of the intelligence services. He listened and took notes.

"Do I need to make a formal complaint?"

"No, it's not worth it. Also, you'll look a bit stupid as you fell for it – you were the one who drove her to the airport, after all."

Indeed.

That afternoon my phone started ringing and didn't stop. An article had been published on the *Parisien* website and reposted on all the nationalist and extreme right sites. I suspected the police on the night shift had tipped off a journalist. The headline had been seen by Sophie's family and mine, and by our friends. My daughters had told my ex-wife. Everyone had seen or read something and wanted to know what was going on. The online comments were revealing. Mostly, they proposed sending Sophie back to where she came from and banning Islam in France.

I had to tell everyone who called that Hugo and Sophie had left for Turkey and that I'd had no news for two days now. Sophie's sister burst into loud sobs. My parents, retired and living in the mountains in eastern France, hung up after a painful silence. Everyone asked me the same questions, again and again. There was nothing I could say. To try and reassure them, I told them, "You know, our intelligence services have the means to plant a camera in a camel's ass to hit a target in the Iraqi desert. There's no need to worry – they'll find them quickly."

But I was kidding myself. The intelligence services had better things to do than help me find my wife and son, apparently. Now I doubt they'd be capable of planting anything anywhere.

That afternoon, the police asked me to return to the station. To make things move faster, they said, it would best for me to make a formal complaint.

"Can I withdraw the charge if she comes back?" I asked.

"Of course, sir."

They refrained from telling me that the withdrawal of a complaint wouldn't mean the prosecution would be discontinued. That decision is up to the prosecutor, and there's rarely leniency when child abduction is involved. But I didn't know that. So I made a complaint against my wife for the kidnap of our son.

The next day I called work and asked to take sick leave. I had to explain what had happened. To say the words, "My wife has left for Syria with our four-year-old son" hurt me more than anything I'd been through so far. I could imagine the sympathy in people's eyes and the questions they didn't dare say aloud. *How had I let her go? How did I not suspect anything?* I understood them. In their place I'd have thought the same thing.

Immediately after this, I called Hugo's school to explain his absence. I was deeply moved by how kind they were. Hugo's teacher asked me if I'd like to drop by and pick up some of his schoolwork.

Sophie's nephew Christophe, Alice's older son, came to help me as soon as he found out what had happened. Together, in my newly cleaned and tidied living room, we called and emailed anyone we could think of: the Quai d'Orsay,[9] the French Ambassador in Turkey, the French Consulate in the closest Turkish town to the Syrian border. If only they could be stopped before they crossed the border! I surfed the internet and scrutinised Facebook. The profiles of the three boys were telling. Over time, they'd gone from posting off-colour jokes and flattering selfies to verses from the Qur'an, first in French and then in Arabic. They had a *surat* for every occasion. They replied to anything and everything by pulling one out of the hat. Then their comments became less frequent. Since they left for Syria, their profiles had been inactive. But through a process of cross-referencing, I found a profile Idriss had opened under another name, and now the tone was completely different. It was a furious rant against the West, littered with nonsensical political comments and propaganda photos. My blood turned cold when I looked at it. What was Sophie thinking by getting mixed up in that? With Christophe, I wrote emails to the French president, François Hollande and Bernard Cazeneuve, the prime minister. I received standard emails in response. I also called all Sophie's former colleagues and learned, again and again, that she'd changed, and that she'd lied to me.

That night, unable to sleep, I watched TV and smoked like a chimney. The first stroke of luck came from my friend Benjamin. We'd both been pastoral school assistants together, and he now worked the media. He put me in touch with Dounia Bouzar, a specialist in Islamist radicalisation. An anthropologist and sociologist, she was also a Muslim who was at the forefront of the fight against the Islamic State's recruitment strategy. I contacted her immediately. It was now nine days that I'd been without any news from my wife and son.

"You're right – there's no point in kidding yourself. She's probably on the way to Syria."

I appreciated her honesty. She went on.

---

9   The French Ministry of Foreign Affairs.

"She'll get in touch with you. That will be the critical point. Above all, don't get angry with her. You mustn't overwhelm her or try to reason with her. That won't work and will only push her further away. Try to look at things like this: a stranger has taken the place of the wife you know and love. You have to bring her back. Keep reminding her of happy memories, of good times you've had together. Hold on to the thought that she might have forgotten everything for now, but it's all still there and not so far beneath the surface. You can try spirituality, too. You need to speak her language."

"That'll be difficult. She knows me well, and there's no bigger rationalist than me. She won't believe it."

"Try all the same, find a way. It's no longer the language of reason that she speaks, but that of the emotions and religious ideology."

"But I don't understand. She used to call them idiots. She said that what they did wasn't true Islam. She was extremely critical of the three boys for going. 'They broke their families' hearts,' she used to say to me. I don't get it."

"You need to understand that she's changed. During the months before she left, she was living a double – even a triple – life. It was like a spy film. She's done everything so that no one will suspect her. She's lied. You need to be brave."

I can't say that any of this was encouraging, but at least I had a plan. I sat down at my computer immediately and wrote Sophie an email. From that moment on, I wrote several times a day. I sent her photos of our marriage, pictures of Hugo in her arms, the picture of her pregnancy test. I talked to her about love, about missing her, about how empty I felt. It was hard to find the words at first – I felt more like screaming at her and ordering her to come back. What I *wanted* to write was, "Bring back Hugo immediately, you lunatic, for heaven's sake!" But I wrote something else entirely.

The strange thing was that, as I wrote the words I hoped would rekindle her feelings and make her see reason, I felt a profound change in myself. I rediscovered our love myself. I went back over the happy times we'd spent together and remembered how close we'd been. Everything which had been fading away, which I'd been forgetting as well. As I tried to win her round, I fell in love with her again.

But the days passed and still there was still silence. I felt like I was going crazy. I stayed away from my family, avoiding everyone with whom things could become emotional. I simply could not deal with the questions and other people's tears any more. I restricted myself to only seeing people who could help me, people who were "doers", like me. Each day brought a new disappointment. Each day, I grew more worried. I never went inside our bedroom; being in there made me too upset. I threw a sleeping bag on the sofa and spent the nights my nights there, dazed, watching tattoo shows on the cable channels. Somehow they calmed me down and helped me forget. I dug out some of Hugo's drawings and put them on the living room table.

Going into his classroom had broken my heart. It was home time and the children were putting on their anoraks. Those staying after school streamed into the playground. Parents were beginning to arrive to pick up the others. Hugo's best friend was there and his mother looked at me with a sad smile. The teacher gave me a bag of Hugo's work, which I took back to the house.

On the tenth day, I received a first, terse message from Sophie telling me that she and Hugo were fine. She had started working at the orphanage, she said, ending with a kiss. I was electrified and stuck to Dounia's advice. I replied that I missed her and Hugo and that the apartment was empty without them. I sent a photo of her when she was pregnant. I told her I'd finished rearranging the living room. How were things for them? My words were loving and tender.

"I didn't know that you still loved me," she replied forlornly.

"I love you so much," I said. "Don't you want to come back?"

"I'd forgotten that photo, you know..."

I understood that she was lost. I could sense her distress and unease. I said they should come home.

"Don't worry, I'll be back," she said and reassured me that Hugo was with her all the time.

I was extremely relieved that she was in Turkey. At all costs, I had to stop her before she crossed the border into Syria. I told myself that, if she hadn't made it there in ten days, perhaps she was hesitant about going. I wrote to her saying that I'd really like see how it was where they were. She promised to send some photos. While I waited, she sent me a voice message from Hugo.

"I love you, papa, I miss you a lot. You're my best friend."

I listened to this on the sofa, crying my eyes out, my legs like jelly.

A little while later, I received a photo of her and Hugo. The two of them filled the frame. But, with Christophe, we were able to enlarge it so as to see something of the background. With the help of Google Earth, I worked out that they were probably in the region of Sanliurfa, in Turkey, close to the Syrian border. It's a beautiful town, a crossroads for trade and religions. We contacted the embassy in Turkey to see if we were right. I faxed them an image. One of our contacts thought he recognised the Ataturk dam on the Euphrates.

I wanted to go immediately. I imagined myself arriving in the city, combing the streets for them with the photo in my hand. I'd bring them back as soon as I found them. But everyone advised against it. My family didn't want me to go for safety reasons, which I didn't want to hear. But the DGSI and Dounia Bouzar both explained to me that my presence could set off a chain reaction of events. This part of Turkey was not secure. A French guy wandering around asking questions about jihadists would attract a lot of attention. If Sophie was there, her contacts on the ground could decide to get her over the border faster. That could be dangerous for her, for me and for Hugo. The frontier zone was infested with supporters of the Islamic State group, spies who were looking out for the enemies of Daesh – in particular members of the Free Syrian Army. Assassinations were common.

Two weeks went by, during which I wrote to Sophie every day. Her absence was unbearable. Communication was difficult; when she managed to call we could only talk for a few minutes before getting cut off, and I could never get through when I called her. She sent a few short emails, sometimes with a photo of Hugo. She spoke to me about her work in the orphanage, but she wouldn't reply to any direct questions. She was reticent and evasive. I was afraid she'd drop off the radar entirely. I didn't know if she was telling me the truth. I didn't know what to believe. But she promised she'd be coming home. I clung onto that.

On 16th March, I received her last message. Then there was nothing. Silence again. Three terrible days of silence. On 19th March, I received an anonymous message.

"Forget your wife and your son, they're in the Islamic State, and they won't be coming back."

I went crazy then. Syria? Daesh? I would never see them again. Could it just be more bullshit? How could I know? It was torture.

Through an old friend from school who'd joined the police, I was able to get hold of the switchboard number of the DGSI and started harassing them.

"A French woman and a child! You have to help me. They might be being held prisoner!"

At the other end of the line, a man gave a deep sigh and answered bluntly.

"You need to stop this, sir and let us get on with our job."

But who would help me? Was it possible they'd be allowed to vanish like that?

Finally Sophie called me. I could barely hear her voice. She was whispering feverishly, speaking very fast.

"Calm down, speak up a bit. I can't understand anything."

She explained she needed medical certificates which would necessitate her return to France on medical grounds. I immediately called a doctor and told him the whole story. He drafted a certificate which I scanned and sent to her. Once again, there was no news. I understood nothing about the story of the certificate.

On 23rd March, Dounia Bouzar invited me to a conference at the Porte de Pantin in Paris that she'd organised on the issue of young French people going to Syria. As I walked into the auditorium, my phone rang. I answered immediately – the phone was always in my hand, as though it was permanently attached there – and rushed outside the room, so I could talk. Sophie was breathless.

"We're in Raqqa. Help us...they won't let me leave..." and then the call cut out. I felt as if my head was exploding. I finally had the confirmation I feared: they were in Syria. Now I knew where. They were alive, which was positive. They were being held there, which was not. By who? How? Where? She hadn't had time to say. What had I sensed from her voice? Relief. Relief that she'd managed to reach me, that I'd picked up the phone. She also sounded very tired and strangely, there was also a kind of calm in her voice. She'd been speaking very fast, because the line could cut out at any moment. But she was calm.

People were coming and going around me. The seminar had started in the auditorium. I looked at the faces in the audience. Mostly they were white families – ordinary French people like me, whose stories I could guess at. A sister, a brother, a son. All had lost someone close, someone who had for some inexplicable reason left to wreak death and destruction on behalf of a terrorist organisation. On each and every worried, attentive face I saw the same thing: incredulity.

As soon as Dounia stepped down from the stage, I hurried over to tell her about the call I'd just received. She introduced me to one of the other participants, from the

Ministry of the Interior.[10] I explained everything to him, and he gave me some advice. But when I said the word "Raqqa," they looked cagey. I knew what they were thinking: that I'd never see my wife and child again.

I let my family know Sophie and Hugo were in Syria. Everyone was flabbergasted. At Sophie's sister's house, they prayed. My sister-in-law chanted, lit candles and sought out help from their church community. She was lucky to have them, but that wasn't going to bring Sophie back.

I kept on writing, hoping she would receive my emails. I wanted her to know I was thinking about her and that I'd do whatever I could. I received a message telling me that she and Hugo were fine, and that no one was harming them. She was waiting for the right time to escape.

Escape? I imagined them in Raqqa. I knew nothing about the place, but I'd seen terrifying images. They wouldn't have a chance. Once more, I decided I'd go looking for them. I could pass myself off as a convert. It would be enough to learn a few *surat*s and some words of Arabic, and to grow my hair and beard. Obviously, if I was found out it could be dangerous – for her and for me. I fantasised about saving her. I was desperate. The silence was unbearable.

I called people every day. My contact at the intelligence service, who'd impressed me when we first met, didn't seem on top of things. I knew both the file and the situation on the ground better. I didn't see how he could help me. As for the police – forget it. The DGSI was tight-lipped and opaque. From the ministries, I had some comforting words but nothing else. I felt as though I was screaming into the void. Basically, no one wanted to go and rescue an alleged terrorist who'd left for *jihad* on her own free will – even when I explained it was as though she'd been brainwashed by a sect. Because this was exactly what it was, this radical Islam, a powerful sect of fanatics. How could anyone talk about free will when she had been indoctrinated by effective prop-

---

10 The French Home Office.

aganda techniques that had been tried and tested over and
over again?

If I was able to arouse any interest at all with my story, it
was because there was a child at stake. Without that, no one
would have replied to me and Sophie would have been lost.

On 10th April, she sent me a message on WhatsApp. She
told me some news about her health; she'd had an operation
for an ovarian cyst, but obviously it hadn't gone well. She'd
had a minor haemorrhage and there was blood in her stomach. She'd had another operation and was in hospital.

There was no news of Hugo. Where was he while she was
in hospital? I was terrified. Sophie was going to die and they
were going take my son. For another 13 days there was no
more news. Nothing. I kept writing and calling. I lay awake
all night, tormented by insomnia. I chain smoked, lighting
each cigarette with the butt of the last one. I no longer felt
alive. I didn't take calls from my parents: their worried questions – echoes of mine – drove me mad. Amoeba larvae lived
more fulfilling lives than I did. I alternated between phases
of insane hope, when I was convinced that something was
going to happen, that they'd come home, that someone
would help me, and moments of despondency so brutal that
it felt like my spirit had capsized. Madness stalked me.
I interrogated myself for hours on end, wracked with guilt.

I went back over everything, again and again. Who was
the person I'd lived with? Did I really know so little about
her? She had lied to me so badly. When I thought about all
the signs I'd missed, I wanted to scream. The distance and
discord between us had blinded me. Things were going
badly and I'd wanted some space. I'd let her slip away from
me. Perhaps I hadn't exactly pushed her, but I'd gone along
with it. So what if she came home late from work? Fine.
I was happy at home with Hugo and once he was tucked up
in bed, I could relax and smoke on the balcony.

I'd been conscious we were no longer a couple, that the
trust between us was gone. The skill she'd used to get round

me and convince me to let her go took my breath away and left me furious.

"How could you have let her take Hugo?" my mother asked me a hundred times.

Her question hit me like a club. It was true. I could not understand how I'd been able to let her go with our four-year-old son without knowing exactly where she was taking him. No address. A dubious, half-baked project. I was ashamed. She had played on my weaknesses and on my tiredness, too. Since she'd been practicing her religion more intensely, and especially since she became so involved with the lives of the families she was working with, she'd slowly turned away from us.

I tormented myself so much I started grinding my teeth. I thought again of the message warning me about Sophie's trip. Why hadn't I called Eric there and then to talk to him about it? The sender's pseudonym had made me think of him ("Jimmy Hendrix," and Eric's surname was Dricks). The style of the message pointed to a young person from the community centre. The spelling was terrible, the syntax confused, and there were capital letters all over the place. At the same time, it was written by someone who felt at ease creating a false identity and an email address which would only be used once. All hallmarks of one of the youths. I should have called Eric.

If I'd called him, I would have known that Sophie had resigned without telling me. She would have been exposed, her projects revealed as a sham and Hugo would still be with me. It was as though I'd been asleep during those months.

I was devastated.

Yet I continued to write to her, to remind her of the happy days we'd shared and to bring them to life in my mind, too. When I wrote to her, I had to supress my animosity and my anger and, strangely, it was as though they then ceased to exist. I was absolutely sincere when I applied the technique Dounia Bouzar had advised. Perhaps I was even more sincere than if I'd allowed myself to be angry. Perhaps it was the same for her. During the last few months, when she had compartmentalised the different parts of her life, she was still sincere, in her own way, in each of them. She was sincere when she sent me the pictures of Hugo in the airplane and when she said she'd see me soon...

One morning, I was standing at the kitchen window when I decided I had to face the truth: they were dead. I would never see them again. Hugo and Sophie were dead. It was over.

That evening, the phone rang. They were alive. In danger, but alive.

17: The Crisis Cell

The blood froze in my veins.

"Is Hugo ok?"

"He's fine. He's playing with the other children here."

"You've got phone reception there?"

"Yes, I can pick up the signal from the cybercafé."

"Don't move. I'll call you back."

I hung up and called my contact at the Ministry of Foreign Affairs on his mobile. I told him the situation. He told me he'd "take note". My wife was in the middle of Raqqa, on the run from the Islamic State and he'd *take note*? Fine. We weren't out of the woods yet.

I'd been outside when the call came and I was still in the street. I picked up the pizza I'd placed on the window sill of a building, then walked quickly towards the house and called the officer from the intelligence service. He also took note. When I got home, I called Benjamin, the friend who'd first put me in touch with Dounia Bouzar. He answered after the first ring.

"Sophie and Hugo are on the run. They're being sheltered by a family, but they can only stay there for one day. The authorities are useless. We have to get them out ourselves."

This was something we'd discussed already. He'd told me about the son of one of his colleagues, a guy called Anton who'd lived in Syria before the war. He was an activist, with contacts in the Free Syrian Army that he maintained from France.

"I'll call Anton," said Benjamin.

I prayed Anton would answer and that he'd help us. I imagined a shady character, a Bob Denard[11] type mercenary, afraid of nothing. An adventurer, who'd reassure me.

Benjamin called me back.

"I've had Anton on the phone. He's with his Syrian friend, Majid. They can get her out, but it usually takes some time. The undercover branch of the Free Syrian Army in Raqqa has to carry out checks to make sure that this isn't a trap to expose them. That happens a lot, apparently. Sophie has to stay for at least two more days where she is."

"I don't think that's going to be possible. The family she's with are terrified."

"Give me Sophie's number, and they can try and speak to her. She has to convince Majid the story is true, or she's screwed. Do you know how she was able to escape? They sounded a bit suspicious about that part of the story."

"I don't know anything. But they have to help her."

"We'll try. But there's something else..."

"What?"

"They've asked for money, to organise everything."

"A lot?"

"30,000 euros."

I was speechless. It was a huge amount.

"It's a complicated operation, even more than usual. First of all, Sophie's black. That makes her easily identifiable. And then there's the fact she needs to get out so fast. They'll need to bribe people. All this has a cost."

I gulped.

"How much time do I have to find the money?"

"They won't work on credit. You have to give them the money before they launch the operation."

"But...I'll never find 30,000 euros in 24 hours!"

I was a teacher. My bank account was always close to zero by the end of the month, and we had no savings. Any spare

---

11 Robert Denard was a French soldier and mercenary, known for fomenting a series of uprisings and coups across Africa from the 1960s-1990s.

cash went into the account we'd opened for Hugo when he was born – which Sophie had emptied when she left.

"You have to try. I'll help you – we can do it."

While Anton and Majid got in touch with Sophie, I started out on my quest to find the money. I contacted my parents. They were terrified and didn't understand what I was asking.

"Is it a ransom? We won't give anything until we see the child. Otherwise, how can we be sure they'll bring them back?"

I tried to explain to them it wasn't a ransom, but that the money was both to finance the rescue operation – which would be expensive – as well as providing funds for the Free Syrian Army. But I wasn't sure of anything myself. I didn't know Anton or Majid, or anything about what was happening on the ground, aside from what I read in the newspapers. My parents had a point – it could be a trap. Maybe we were going to be fleeced. But it was our only chance, the first ray of hope for several weeks. I was ready to risk it. Reluctantly, my father gave me the small nest egg he'd put aside for his retirement.

I borrowed several hundred euros from colleague, who knew what was going on. I felt like banging my head against the wall – I'd only managed to find 4,000 euros out of the 30,000 I needed. Ideas of varying degrees of craziness went through my head. Rob a bank? Sell all our furniture? Take out a loan? But what could I do in 24 hours?

The next day I went for a meeting in the south of Paris, in the house would become our crisis cell. I knocked at the door and a skinny young guy in his early 20s answered.

"Julien?" He smiled at me. "I'm Anton."

I was stunned. Anton? My saviour? He was more like a student than a spy.

"You weren't expecting me to look like this?"

"Anton! How can I thank you?" I stammered. "No, I wasn't expecting someone like you. But you have my eternal gratitude."

We went inside. Majid was around the same age, a refugee studying journalism in France. He didn't look like Rambo either. But there they were, brave and committed. The only ones ready to help us.

"We're going to help your wife," said Majid. "I've spoken to her, and I believe her. She begged me to help her, and she wasn't lying. I've convinced my contacts on the ground that it's not a trap. They're going to get her out of there."

Then Benjamin arrived, with a sports bag in one hand.

"I had a whip round," he said with an air of victory.

We gathered in the kitchen and he emptied the bag on the table. It was full of the cash he'd been able to get from people he knew professionally. I added the 4,000 euros from my friends, some of it in 20 and 50 euro notes. We sat around the table; Anton and Majid, whose phones vibrated every five minutes, Benjamin and me. We divided up the money.

I felt emotional as I looked at our motley crew – an odd mix of people, united by a common goal. I thought that we must look like drug traffickers or bank robbers, dividing our loot. There were notes of all sizes and even some coins. People had written their names on the envelopes. We counted, then counted again. If only there was enough...

There was 28,000 euros. A huge amount.

But not enough.

At that moment, my phone rang. It was my younger brother.

"Julien, get ready, I've got some good news!"

His brother-in-law, a property entrepreneur, was at a business lunch when he heard about Sophie's situation. He told his colleagues, and they immediately put their hands in their pockets: that evening, my brother brought over 12,000 euros gathered over one meal from people who didn't even know us. I was bowled over by the generosity of those who'd stuck their necks out for us. Majid gave the signal to his contacts on the ground that they could start the rescue. He and Anton, who spoke fluent Arabic, were the intermediaries between Sophie – still hiding out with the family – and the Free Syrian Army undercover agents in Raqqa.

Majid told me he knew the neighbourhood where Sophie was staying. He used to live there himself with his parents, before they'd been driven out by the war, forced to flee because of his political activities. The neighbourhood had been home to Syrian intellectuals, but now was crawling with members of Daesh – fanatics from all over the world, living in homes confiscated by the Islamic State.

"They're right to be afraid," said Majid, talking about the family that was sheltering Sophie. "They're risking their lives for your wife. I've spoken to them. They said they don't want to throw her out, but we need to act quickly. The building is full of mujaheddin – they could be caught at any moment."

Here in this big house, surrounded by these people, I was going to live through my wife and son's escape on the other side of the world, minute by minute. I was powerless and could barely breathe. I knew that a man from the Free Syrian Army would be waiting for Sophie in front of the women's hospital at 7pm.

I waited, trembling.

The two of us were sitting in the living room. The man I'd spoken to on the telephone had told me his name was Majid.

"I'm going to help you," he promised.

I believed him. I had no idea who he was, nor how Julien had met him. I hadn't thought to ask. It wasn't important. He asked for a lot of details about where we were staying and how we'd escaped. I sensed he was weighing up every word. His wariness and prudence were essential for his friends' survival. I made sure I gave him every scrap of information I had, as precisely as I could. When I described the neighbourhood, he told me he used to live there with his parents, "before". Behind this simple word there lay a war and an exile. When we finished talking, he promised to call me back. I waited. The phone rested on the sofa between the woman and myself. As we waited, she seemed as anxious as me. Fear hung in the living room like the smell of a dead animal.

The telephone was silent.

"You can stay here one more day, if you have to. I'm not going to throw you out," she whispered to me. I nodded my head. Her kindness was as great as her fear.

Finally the phone rang. I picked it up before the end of the first ring. The phone was my lifeline.

"Hello? Hello?" I recognised Majid's voice.

"Sophie, they're coming to get you out. You need to go to back to the Daesh hospital. Wait there. A man will come. He'll say my name. You have to follow him."

He spoke in English. I was worried in case I hadn't understood correctly. I made him repeat himself several times.

"How will he recognise me?"

"Perhaps Hugo have something to identify you? How is he dressed?"

Hugo's clothes were terribly faded, with nothing that stood out. I spotted a child's white waistcoat lying on the back of a chair. Madana saw what I was looking at and understood immediately. She nodded and handed it to me.

"He'll be wearing a white waistcoat."

"Great, that's perfect."

"But do you mean now? I should leave now?"

"Yes, it's the time."

I hung up. For a few seconds I was shaking like a leaf. I looked down at my hands. I couldn't stop them from trembling and thought, *my God, I'll never make it.* Then the shakes passed as suddenly as they'd arrived. I stood up, as did Madana. Impulsively, she took me in her arms and hugged me tightly.

"Give me your number. I'll call in a few days to find out if you've managed to get out. I'll pray for you." She didn't give me hers. If we were stopped and I had it with me, it could give her away.

I told Hugo we were leaving.

"You have to be very brave and very, very good. We're going back to papa, but the bad people want to stop us."

Hugo stamped his foot angrily.

"No one's going to stop me seeing my papa!"

"I know. But for that to happen, you have to do everything I say. Understand?"

He nodded his head, looking serious.

I pulled on my niqab and Hugo put on the white waistcoat. It was after 9pm. Darkness had spread over the town. It was late for a woman to be out walking alone in the street, and I hoped I'd find the man quickly. Madana was kneeling at the entrance of the apartment, tears streaming down her face as she kissed Hugo. We hugged each other one last time.

I crept down the stairs, terrified of bumping into the boys. But the place was deserted. My feet slid across the tiles of the large hallway. Then we were in the street. Once again, I felt as if I was both invisible and on display. An anonymous silhouette gliding past the walls. A woman alone in the night.

Hugo walked fast, despite his tiredness. His little legs hurried along, his hand gripping mine tightly. We hurried towards the hospital. There was always some traffic around there as it was a busy road. There were some taxis, parked a bit ahead of us. A small group of men stood in front of the steps outside the hospital, deep in conversation. I stopped at some distance from them and waited, looking anxiously around me through my veil. Some of the men had noticed me. If I stayed there for too long it would look suspicious, and they might come over.

How could I know who was there to save me? He'd look like anyone else – in fact, he'd probably be disguised as an Islamic State sympathiser.

"I'm tired," sighed Hugo, in a small voice.

"Shhh..."

No one came.

We'd already been waiting there for ten minutes. Discreetly, I checked my phone. But from here I couldn't latch onto the signal from the cybercafé. Had I misunderstood where I was supposed to come to? Had something happened to him?

From the corner of my eye, I noticed that one of the men had peeled away from the group and was coming towards us. I moved off immediately. With Hugo's hand held tightly in mine, I started back in the direction of the apartments, my eyes fixed on my phone. I was waiting until we entered the wifi zone of the cybercafé. The moment the icon on my mobile lit up, I called Majid.

"There's no one there! Majid, he isn't there! I'm going to get arrested."

"Sophie, where are you?"

"We were in front of the hospital, but he didn't come."

"Ok, I don't understand. I just had him on the line and he's been looking for you everywhere. Go back to where you were before!"

I hung up.

"Mama, I'm tired." Hugo was on the edge of tears. I took him in my arms and turned back towards the hospital, almost tripping over twice on the uneven pavement. When we got back in view of the hospital, I was relieved to see that the small group of men, who'd been waiting at the foot of the steps, had gone. We waited in front of the hospital again, clearly visible. It was almost pitch black now. No one came.

I stood on the edge of the pavement. I'd be noticed by someone soon. He hadn't come. We'd missed our chance. The despondency rose like an icy wave inside me. I wished I could just give up, but it was impossible because I had Hugo with me. I had to keep going. A motorbike passed us, the driver staring at me. One of Daesh's men. I had to get back to the apartment – I'd ask Madana if we could stay, just for one more night. Perhaps we could reorganise something for tomorrow. With Hugo in my arms, I started walking back the way we'd come.

"Are we going to see papa?" he whispered in my ear. My throat was tight. I stopped at a pedestrian crossing, unable to reply, when I felt a presence behind me. There was a man there. It was over.

He drew up beside me, and without turning his head he muttered, "Majid."

"Oui...yes!"

Tears of joy began to flow from my eyes. The man turned towards me. He was very young. I could make out a pair of large, dark eyes which shone – in all situations, I would learn – with a smile. He leaned over and took Hugo gently from me. Hugo rested his head on the shoulder of this strange man, closed his eyes and fell asleep. With his free hand, he reached out for mine and led me away. I was saved.

We walked along without saying anything for several streets, then he hailed a taxi. I got in the back. He exchanged a few words with the driver during the ride, but I didn't understand anything. Finally, he told the driver to stop and we got out. The neighbourhood we were in was still being built, one charmless building after another rising up from the ground. We walked through the deserted streets for a couple of minutes, then stopped outside a modern building. We went inside and, as always in Raqqa, walked up to the fifth floor. The man opened the door of an apartment and locked it behind us. He put Hugo down – still fast asleep – on a mattress in the corner of the room, then turned towards me with a wide smile.

"You can relax now, my sister! We'll stay here tonight. I'll go and find something to eat. How about chicken and chips?"

Incapable of speaking, I nodded my head and he went out again, leaving me on my own. The apartment was almost empty. There were a few mattresses on the tiled floor and a television in the corner, nothing else. I pulled off my niqab.

When he came back, my saviour encouraged me remove my headscarf. He didn't care about me covering my hair. We sat cross legged on the floor together and shared our meal, talking about one thing or the other, but not the situation we were in. All I learned from Malik – which was not his real name – was that he was 25 years old and married. I would only learn his true story when I got back to France. He'd been a student when the revolution started and had taken part in the protests which swept through the country. For the past five years he'd been fighting as part of a small group of rebels that remained secretly in Raqqa when the Islamic State had taken power. Like his comrades in the resistance, he disguised himself as an extremist, wearing his hair and beard long. These men worked undercover, carrying out whatever sabotage they could. Most of all, they specialised in helping people escape.

That night, though, we just spoke about France as well as his favourite TV programmes. When Hugo woke up, Malik played with him and made him laugh. Then he switched on the TV, which picked up Western channels by satellite. I'd never been a great fan of the small screen, but it was with immense pleasure that I let myself be absorbed by a programme which didn't end with a beheading. Then Malik took a picture of me and asked me to hold a sign covered with writing I couldn't read. Just like the hostages obliged to brandish their captors' demands, I proudly held it up with a big smile. He sent the picture to Majid, who would forward it to Julien. Then he lit a shisha and offered it to me.

"You're crazy, it's forbidden! If we're caught, we'll be whipped in public!"

He burst out laughing.

"If only this was all we had to worry about!"

I needed to rest – the next day was the beginning of a long journey. Malik explained that we would leave in a convoy for the Turkish border. One car would go ahead of us. If they spotted one of the mobile checkpoints they'd alert the car behind us, which would try to catch up with us and stop us. If this didn't work, they'd use their weapons. Malik said this with the fatalism of someone who had lived through war for a long time. We would be in the middle of the convoy, on the motorbike. Malik gave me a travel document belonging to his wife. So long as no one asked me to lift my veil, it would be ok. He impressed on me that I shouldn't speak a word; while foreign fighters often took women from the local population, Syrian men did not have relationships with foreigners, and we'd be discovered immediately if I was seen. I nodded. Hugo and I would be as silent as the grave. I stretched out while he smoked, lost in his thoughts. I was worried I wouldn't be able to sleep a wink that night, thinking about the risks awaiting us the following day. But before I could put this into words, I fell into a deep slumber.

19: The Road

So it was that I found myself back on the dusty road, riding pillion behind Malik on a motorbike, with Hugo on my knees, hidden under my niqab. We'd managed to leave Raqqa without difficulty. Malik knew the permanent checkpoints on the routes out of the town, and I think he'd greased some palms because they spent little time checking us. Afterwards, we drove on without a hitch. Mujaheddin heading for battle sped past in the opposite direction. The road was long, and my back hurt from the jolts. I held Hugo so tightly that my arms were burning.

Suddenly the motorbike bounced over a pothole and flew up into the air, then hit the road again with a bump. Had I dozed off without realising it? My grip around Malik's chest had loosened, and with horror I realised I was sliding backwards. I was couldn't hold on any more, and I couldn't let go of Hugo to straighten myself up again. I realised I was going to fall. I wrapped myself around my son's body, to break his fall.

I flew off the back of the bike in a sitting position, and my coccyx slammed into the asphalt. A sharp pain shot up my spine. Hugo screamed in terror. I tried to extricate myself from under my veil to see if he was ok, without exposing myself too much. Malik slammed on the brakes a few metres ahead, then ran over to us in a panic.

"Is the boy ok?"

I comforted Hugo, who was unhurt. But I couldn't get up. Malik looked around us, worriedly.

"We need to get moving. We can't stay here."

He took me by the arm and helped me up. I held back a cry. It felt like I'd fractured my tailbone, at the very least. Malik helped me walk back to the motorbike and to get back on. He seemed anxious.

"Can you hold on? Can you manage?"

Yes, I could hold on. Tears of pain streamed down my face under my veil as he restarted the bike. I could tell he was doing his best to drive as carefully as possible and to avoid the bumps, but the slightest vibration from the engine caused such agony that I had to bite my lips to stop myself crying out.

"Are you ok, mama?" asked Hugo, from under my abaya. Now he was awake he held his arms around me, which helped.

"Yes, mama's fine."

The motorbike sped onwards. Malik explained that there were eight fixed checkpoints on the way to the border. We could avoid all of them bar one, which was on a road we couldn't circumvent. There was no other way possible. Although he never stopped smiling, his worried tone of voice told me that this was the unknown factor in our journey. I began to pray.

"Save Hugo. Let Hugo see his father again. I made a mistake, please don't let him be punished for it." I don't know whom I was begging with such fervour, but it made me feel better.

We hastened towards the border. As we approached the unavoidable check-point, Malik slowed down. The car ahead of us had gone through. The guard on duty suddenly turned around and went into the sentry box. Through the window, I saw him pick up a bottle of water and take several large gulps, totally uninterested in the traffic. He was alone. The way ahead was clear. Malik put his foot on the gas, and we passed through at full speed. Someone had protected us. Feverishly, I murmured words of gratitude and praise. We were only a few kilometres from the frontier.

We stopped in front of a hut in the Tal Abiad district. Malik parked the motorbike, took Hugo in his arms and helped me walk inside. I was limping and the pain was terrible. I couldn't sit, so I stayed standing and leaned against a wall. Malik left us for a short while, to go and get some food from some friends of his who lived nearby. When he came back, he played with Hugo while shooting me concerned looks. He insisted I eat something, but I couldn't swallow – the food wouldn't go down.

"Have courage, my sister. It's going to be fine." I nodded my head.

Finally, a man knocked on the door and we were on our way. We were about to cross the border. I looked around me at the bleak landscape, and the barbed wire that stretched out into the distance. I saw neither soldiers nor police. Other fugitives appeared – where they came from, I don't know. It was a no man's land through which dozens of people, leaving from who knows where, surged forward, soon at a run.

Wire cutters came out and the barbed wire was dealt with. Malik lifted Hugo onto his shoulders. I saw my little boy looking down on the crowd, and I forced myself to keep going. On the other side of the barbed wire, there was a muddy trench. As I climbed across the fence, I felt something pulling at me: my *niqab* had got caught in the barbed wire. I jerked at it as the other people jostled around me, and panicked as I felt the cloth slide from my head. There was nothing I could do. I yanked again, hard, and the veil tore, leaving my head and face uncovered. The fresh air was invigorating and gave me energy, but I had trouble keeping up with the others. My feet slipped on the mud and I felt myself lose one shoe, then another. It was impossible to go back, so I kept going with my bare feet. I ran. I fell. I got back up again. The crowd kept going in an unimaginable scramble, pushing and jostling, yet completely silent. Everyone was running for their lives. I desperately fixed my eyes on Hugo's little head and drove myself onwards.

We were in Turkey.

My feet were bleeding. I managed to catch up with Malik and was staggering behind him. Hugo was still on his shoulders. Malik held me by the arms and urged me to keep going. I was exhausted.

"Run, Cinderella, run!"

I raised my head, astonished. He looked at me with that smile of his, and I couldn't stop myself from laughing. He had a point – with my torn muddy stockings, my ragged *niqab* and wild hair, I was quite the Cinderella.

"So where is my carriage?" I asked him.

He burst out laughing.

"Not far, not far. One last push!"

We walked across empty fields. Local Turks in each of the houses bordering them were taking people in. Malik pointed out a small farm. We had reached our destination.

Inside, I was given something to wash my feet with. I had some deep cuts. Malik offered me his trainers. I refused, but he insisted: I wouldn't go far with my feet in that state, he said. His shoes were far too big, and I looked like a clown. He teased me, making Hugo laugh. A taxi came to pick us up and take us to Gaziantep. Night fell over the countryside. I could hardly believe that we'd got out of there. Yet we'd done it. We'd escaped from Syria.

After about half an hour's drive, Malik signalled for the driver to stop. We changed cars. Even on this side of the border, the security rules remained strict. There were a lot of targeted attacks and Syrians in exile who opposed the Islamic State had to stay hidden. Two men around fifty years old were waiting for us in the next car. One was commander of the Free Syrian Army's secret brigade in Raqqa; it was he who'd organised our escape. The other was an exiled Syrian, in whose house we would stay. The three of them smoked like chimneys. Hugo and I found it hard to breathe, but I didn't want to annoy our saviours by complaining. I half opened a window and told myself that it was a small thing to bear now we were safe. I repeated the word again: *safe*. But

I didn't yet feel the relief I'd hoped for. There was still a ball of tension deep in my stomach.

We dropped Malik off somewhere. He was going to rest a bit, then leave to fight again. I hugged him, crying. I would never see him again. On impulse, I searched in the lining of my bag, where I'd hidden my French currency and tried to give him some notes. Embarrassed, he refused firmly then leaned over and hugged Hugo, who he'd carried like his own child. I gave him back his shoes, as we laughed and cried at the same time. My gratitude was total. He walked off, full of courage, towards his destiny. From behind, he seemed so fragile.

Finally, we arrived at the apartment where we would shelter for the night. A small, round woman with a cheerful face greeted us with enthusiasm and generosity. She showed me to the bathroom and gave Hugo and Is some toiletries, all the while berating her husband about something or the other. Then she went to the kitchen to prepare some food and drink.

It was our first shower since we'd been freed. I started at my emaciated body in the mirror, which was soon covered with mud. My hair was dry and had grown a lot since my last haircut, when it had been dyed red. My shoulders were so thin that my head looked enormous and too heavy for my frame. I was frightened by the state I was in. I washed carefully, scrubbing away to rid myself of the dirt from the journey, the tears and the terror of Syria. I washed Hugo just as thoroughly. Then we put on the clothes out hostess had left out for us – a pink tracksuit for me, a red one for Hugo.

We talked until late, in the living room. My hosts, who'd had to flee Syria because of the war, pressed me with questions about the state of Raqqa and about my story. We drank Turkish coffee, thick and bitter, which didn't stop me falling asleep with Hugo in my arms, in the middle of everyone, with the lights on, in the noise and the smoke. The tension was finally evaporating and there was only the pain in my back, my feet and in my shoulder, which ached from holding

Hugo against me during the ride. My body was a mass of injuries, but I slept, soothed by the Arabic conversation going on around me, and I was barely aware of the cover my hostess pulled over us.

20: The Homecoming

The next evening, Julien walked into the bedroom, where Hugo had just fallen asleep. I even didn't manage to get up. In two steps, he leapt across the room and took me in his arms. I could see he was crying, but I didn't have the energy myself. I'd escaped from hell. I knew this with even more certainty now my husband's arms were wrapped tightly around me. Then he picked up Hugo, who hadn't woken up when he came in. He held his son lovingly, and I wanted to beg his forgiveness but I couldn't find words strong enough to express what I wanted to say.

"You've got some explaining to do, Sophie," he said, through his tears.

The three of us left the room and he introduced me to Anton, my saviour. They'd payed the funds over for my rescue. My liberators explained why the price had been so high; the urgency of the operation made it more complicated to carry out, which meant it was more expensive. They seemed almost embarrassed to accept the money. Anton said they were disappointed that it wasn't the French security services that had come to collect us. They had hoped to prove to the French that there was a still a resistance in Syria capable of organising undercover operations, even from the heart of the Islamic State's capital city. The rebels had been fighting alone for a long time.

We took leave of our hosts. Exceptional circumstances had created an exceptional bond between us; the young woman of the house and I hugged each other as though we'd known each other all our lives. I was sad at the thought of leaving them. We felt so close to each other at that moment.

I had trouble putting some shoes on. The wounds were infected and swollen. Leaning against Julien, we climbed into a taxi which took us to the Holiday Inn next to the airport. When we got there, we met with French consular representatives and two Turkish police inspectors. While Julien took the still sleeping Hugo to the bedroom, I sat in the deserted dining room and answered questions – not about my own story, but about Raqqa. They made me repeat the names of all the people I could remember meeting there and asked me to describe all the areas and places I'd been to. It was late when they left. I went upstairs to bed.

The next morning, I felt a little hand shaking my shoulder. It was Hugo, standing at my head.

"Mama, mama, is that papa?" He couldn't believe it. I burst out laughing. Delirious with joy, Hugo threw himself on his father, whispering excitedly.

"I'm never going to leave you again, papa."

From that moment, he didn't leave his father's side.

We left for the airport. As I hadn't been able to get our passports back, I could only travel with a paper given me by the Consulate – a kind of travel document. The diplomat I'd met the evening before was at the airport to make sure everything went according to plan.

We flew to Istanbul without too much trouble. When we arrived, a customs official held us back. I'd been instructed not to admit I'd come from Syria. Repentant *jihadists* were usually locked up in Turkish prisons if the police managed to get their hands on them. But after a little discussion and a call to the Consulate which had provided our travel documents, we were allowed to go.

I felt sad and empty in the plane, overwhelmed from the emotions of the past few days. I wondered what would be waiting for me when I got home. I was going to have to explain myself, no getting away from that. I thought about my sister and my nieces. I thought about Julien, who was holding my hand. It was overwhelming. We began our descent to Paris. I pictured my house in my head. Life was going to start again.

It took ages to get out of the plane, with the other passengers shuffling ahead of us. Then we turned a corner and saw the reason for the hold up: a police check at the end of the tunnel. I realised it was there for me. I swallowed.

My turn came.

"Your papers, madam."

I handed over the paper from the Consulate. One of the officers examined it, then looked around at the woman standing behind him.

"If you wouldn't mind stepping to one side, madam. We are from the Ministry of the Interior[12] and request that you follow us."

I tried not to notice as the other passengers stared at me. The woman checked Julien and Hugo's papers.

"Since the father is here, I'll allow your son to go with him. You seem to be calm enough, so I'm not going to handcuff you – but you need to promise you'll behave yourself. Are you going to be reasonable?"

I nodded my head.

"Can I kiss my son?"

She let me. I said goodbye to Julien and Hugo, then followed the three officers from the DGSI.

---

12 The equivalent of the British Home Office.

I was taken into custody at the headquarters of the DGSI in Levallois-Perret, were I could be kept for up to 96 hours. They took my phone, my jacket and my money. I refused the offer of a lawyer as I didn't see how it would help me. I waited in a small cell for my interrogation. It was clean, but cold. Everything was fixed to the floor. There was a paper blanket on the concrete bed. My head was empty. I had no idea what I was facing.

They came to get me, and I was handcuffed for the first time in my life. But I was so dazed from everything I'd been through that I felt nothing. My body was indifferent to the pain and the discomfort. I felt a profound sense of detachment. All I could think was that I needed to see my loved ones and seek their forgiveness.

I walked down the corridor, my hands behind my back. The other cells were occupied too – by men, going by the size of the trainers left outside the doors. We arrived at an office, where an agent was waiting for me. He sat me down, removed the handcuffs and the interrogation began. For the first time, I told the whole story of my journey from the community centre to Raqqa. I answered all the questions, taking time to think when I wasn't sure. I told him everything.

They took me back to the cell. I was very tired and stretched out on the bed, but it was hard to sleep. I wanted to go home.

Four hours later, they came for me again. The handcuffs came out, and I went through it all once more; I sat in front of the same agent and we started from the beginning. He made me repeat my story from start to finish. Some new details came back to me, and he probed me on certain points. Just like the Turkish police, it was the facts that interested him – he wanted names, dates and places. I replied to all his questions, then they brought me back to my cell. I accepted some food – an apple and some biscuits – but I still had huge problems swallowing. I had no concept of time. There was no window and I had no watch. I waited. Once again, they came to fetch me for another interrogation.

I would spend two days at the DGSI – 48 hours – and be questioned eight times. On the first day, the agent was kind and considerate. One the second, I had another one who was cold and disdainful. But the questions were always the same and went on and on, one after the other. By the second day, my answers were shorter – I'd already told them everything, and the new officer was frankly hostile. But I stayed calm and polite. I heard cries from the other cells, but couldn't make out what they were saying.

Finally, they told me I was leaving. An agent came with me to the entrance of the building.

"How am I going to get back home? Have you informed my husband?" I asked.

"Don't worry, we'll take care of everything."

And indeed they did. A police car from Élancourt police station was waiting for me outside the door.

"An allegation has been lodged against you for the abduction of your child. We're taking you to court now."

I was dumbfounded.

We sped to the court at Versailles, lights flashing. When we got there I was put in another cell, a filthy hole with walls covered in vomit and dried excrement. The smell was so vile I couldn't breathe, but I tried to put things into perspective. Just four days ago, I'd escaped from prison in Raqqa. I'd seen a lot worse.

After about 20 minutes, I was taken from the cell, still with my hands cuffed behind my back and led to a room where a young defence lawyer was waiting for me. We had a short time to prepare for my hearing in front of the judge. I was alarmed by the young woman's lack of knowledge. She didn't know anything about my case, or have all the necessary information in my file, and I had a feeling she wasn't going to be very useful. After ten minutes, she felt she knew enough and they took me back to the cell. It seemed like a parody of justice. I couldn't see how anyone could do their job correctly in these conditions – how could the lawyer defend me if she didn't know anything about me?

Finally, it was time to go in front of the magistrate. I went into the courtroom. I was in a total state, exhausted and disoriented. The clerk read out the charges. I listened, hearing the words but understanding nothing. It was difficult to believe they were talking about me. The judge asked me several questions, which I answered as best I could. My lawyer didn't say a word. She still hadn't said anything by the time they took me back to my cell. This time I didn't notice the dirt. I was trying to understand what had just happened. But after only a few minutes – and I immediately guessed this wasn't a good sign – the agent came to get me again. The judge gave her verdict: she had decided I should be detained in a *maison d'arrêt*[13] for a period not exceeding four months. I was stunned. I'd only just gained my freedom and was now going to be locked up again. Distraught, I turned to my lawyer.

"Would you like to challenge the decision?" the judge asked me.

I nodded. They took me straight to the office of another judge, for some kind of immediate appeal hearing. The public prosecutor's representative spoke first, launching into an elaborate account of the dangerous situation into which I'd dragged my son. Behind this, I knew, lurked the spectre of Islamist terrorism. Notwithstanding the actual charge, it seemed clear that they were more interested in punishing me than protecting Hugo.

I took the floor and made my plea with all the strength of my convictions.

"I'm not dangerous. I made a mistake, a serious mistake, at a moment in my life when I was very fragile. I deeply regret any pain I may have caused. But I'm not dangerous, I've never participated in any violent act – on the contrary, I was held there against my will. I need to be with my child and he needs his mother. We all want to be together again – my husband would tell you this himself, if he was here."

"My colleague's decision is upheld," the judge ruled. "You will be detained at the *maison d'arrêt* in Versailles immediately. It's a good place – you'll see."

I was crying all the tears I had in my body. I couldn't believe my ears: I was sure I'd be leaving straight away. I had nothing to apologise for, except for what I'd put my loved ones through. I'd been a victim of grooming, I'd been abused, I'd got myself out of there at the risk of my life, and

---

13 *Maison d'arrêts* are a category of prisons in France, in Belgium and other French-speaking countries, which hold prisoners awaiting trial or sentencing, or those being held for less than one year, similar to county jails in the United States.

they were locking me up? I couldn't believe it. Would I have been treated like this if I'd got mixed up with a cult? As I sobbed, I scribbled down the Julien's number, held it out to the lawyer and asked her to tell him what had happened.

The police drove me to the *maison d'arrêt*, which was next door to the courthouse. It was a vast building I'd often passed by without ever wondering about the women inside. This time the heavy metal gates clanked open for me and swallowed me up. Swipe cards, used instead of keys, bleeped at every door. Still in tears, I found myself in front of the guard in charge of admissions, a handsome, fit looking guy with blond hair. I'd soon learn that he'd been nicknamed "Brad Pitt" by the inmates. He had very bright eyes and a gentle manner. He handed me some tissues.

"Come on, it's not so bad – you'll see. Some of the prisoners here are very nice girls. It'll be fine..."

I sobbed even harder. I was going to be locked in a cell with criminals – murderers, even. They gave me an ID number, and I became a prisoner.

I spent the first few days in a cell with other new arrivals. It was in an observation area where prison staff could assess the characters of new inmates before they were moved into the general population, so this could be done as smoothly as possible. I shared this space with another new girl, a small woman with a very serene manner. She told me calmly that she'd killed her husband. I didn't close my eyes all night, and refused the food and medication offered. I felt cornered. The next day, I had an interview with the Prison Director.

"I'm going to put you in a nice cell, with some kind women. Keep your head down, don't tell your life story to the world, and everything will be fine. Keep yourself to yourself and don't answer any questions."

There were six of us in a cell designed for two. But I didn't meet prisoners, I met friends who were facing adversity, who welcomed me and took care of me when I was too weak and dejected to do it myself, asking nothing in return. We did everything to bring some humanity into our relationships, fighting all the time against the dehumanisation bred into the prison system.

Chloé was 20 years old. Born into a poor family in northern France, she'd been raped by her stepfather when she was 13 years old and had run away from home. She'd lived on the street where she'd been through some very tough times. She'd taken a lot of drugs and had a child that had been taken away from her. Then she'd fallen in love with Cédric, a *Ch'ti*[14] like her, who sometimes hit her when he was high on drugs, but whom she loved madly. She'd committed violent burglaries with him. They were both in prison, but all she dreamed of was being reunited with him again.

Chloé was the only one in our cell who had a job in the workshop. She shared her money with the rest of us, bought us stuff from the canteen and sung us the hits from *Nouvelle Star*.[15] She knew everything that went on in the prison. Her only vice – that we were aware of – was her addiction to the soap opera, *Plus Bell la Vie*,[16] which she watched religiously every evening. Out of respect for her, we all kept silent at this time. She was pregnant. When the baby was born, she'd be sent to Fresnes prison where there was a nursery. She'd be able to keep him until he was six months old. I didn't know what would become of the child after that.

Rona wasn't even 25 years old. She'd been born into a travelling community and was in prison for assault. She was the only one among us who'd been convicted of a serious crime, rather than a misdemeanour. Her 18 year-old younger brother had been raped and beaten by one of their acquaintances during a drunken party. Rona and her cousins avenged her brother by catching his attacker, beating him almost to death, then releasing him for a ransom. She had an extremely kind nature.

---

14 A dialect of French from the North East of the country. The term is also used to refer to the inhabitants of the area.

15 French TV show based on Pop Idol.

16 Soap opera portraying the everyday lives of residents in Mistral, a working-class neighbourhood in Marseille.

Marianne was 60 years old, but told everyone she was 43. She was a big woman, cheerful and proud, who was a complete nymphomaniac. Of Cameroonian and Congolese heritage, she was a fervent Catholic who belted out hymns at the top of her voice while she did the cleaning. She'd been accused of committing large scale child benefit fraud, but swore her innocence. She was warm and generous, but snored so loudly at night you could almost feel the walls shaking.

Charline was a student from a good family, who hadn't dared to disappoint her parents. She'd fallen in love with the wrong type of guy, and had committed a series of frauds with him. She was so ashamed of being in prison that she'd told her parents she was studying overseas in a seminary for a year. She never had any visitors.

Every morning at 7am, the guards came round to check everyone was still there, and that no one had hanged themselves. The more easy-going ones were satisfied with a wave of the hand, while others insisted we get up and come to the door. This would put Chloé in a very bad temper, and we took turns calming her down. This was also when we'd be given bread for the day. Other than Brad Pitt, we called the guards Barbie, Cruella and Kaput.

Despite the overcrowding, we kept our cell immaculate as we were all fanatical about cleaning. Chloé took advantage of her pregnancy-induced insomnia by scrubbing the corners of the room when she couldn't sleep. Together we kept the place shipshape.

There was no absence of religion in our cell. I didn't talk about Islam to anyone except Chloé, who was also a convert and prayed regularly. Marianne, between hymns, told us her husband was Jewish. But although we never challenged what she said (this had the immediate effect of making her burst into tears) none of us believed a word she told us.

Charline's family was Christian. Like me, she spoke little about herself, and I didn't know exactly what she'd done to end up there. But Chloé, Rona and Marianne made enough noise for all of us. The sixth cellmate, Hope, was a Nigerian who'd been arrested for pimping as part of an organised crime ring. She was 34 years old and you had the feeling that she'd already experienced more than most people do in a lifetime.

The terms under which I was detained were very strict and prohibited me from communicating with my family, including Julien. I didn't have any visits, and I wasn't allowed to use the telephone. My money had never been returned to me, so I couldn't buy anything. In prison, everything costs money and nothing is cheap. I didn't know know what Julien knew – I later learned that no one told him anything, and that he came several times to the prison with Hugo asking to see me, or simply to ask for news.He wrote to me every day, but the judge had forbidden me from receiving mail during my first month in prison.

I didn't leave the cell much. I heard to arguments and savage fights going on outside and didn't much feel like finding myself in the middle of them. The women tried to persuade me to go out as they didn't think it was healthy to stay inside all the time. If only they knew. They went regularly to the library, the exercise yard, the gym...Crafty and resourceful, they knew everything that was going on. These were women used to surviving, and their ability to adapt was impressive.

I spent long hours stretched out on my bed. I read and wrote a lot. I cried constantly when I was alone, as though I was ridding myself of all the anger and fear of the past few months through my tears. During these hours, I went over and over the chain of events. I tried to understand what had happened to me.

At the end of the first month, I was finally allowed mail and received my first letters from Julien. On the advice of another prisoner, I'd hired a young lawyer from a large firm. Jihadism was in the news and my case was interesting for him. Unfortunately, my request for early release was refused.

I read and I reflected on everything. I wrote to Julien, to my sister, to my nieces. The rift inside in me was always there; I could sense it and see it. I explored it more deeply than ever now that I knew it would never entirely close. I hoped that by recognising it, I would never again allow a religion, an ideology or an individual to get inside and manipulate me.

I left the *maison d'arrêt* in Versailles in June 2015, after two months, to go home to my son and husband. I said goodbye to my companions, who had spent the past weeks gently trying to help me get back on my feet without asking too many questions. I would probably never see any of them again – just like I would never see Malik, who saved me, Madana, who sheltered Hugo and me, Souria, who cooked pasta for my son and feared how the images of torture would affect her unborn child, Houda, who fed me and gave me the pink tracksuit, and Anton and Majid, without whom nothing would have been possible.

I would like to pay tribute to those who helped me, those who took risks for us, those who didn't judge me – even if they didn't always understand me. My heart will always be with those, in Syria, in Turkey or in France, who helped us back to freedom. I also wish to thank my family and my friends who, after our return, formed an unbreakable human shield around us, which rescued me when my morale was at rock bottom. Thank you to those who understand that depression is not a choice, a way of life or a weakness of character, but a terrible illness.

A little time after I was released from prison, I learned that Idriss and Mohammed died in combat. Their families received a letter affirming this. As for Suleymane, no one knows what happened to him.

Other Books Published by First Draft Publishing

I am Akbar Agha: Memories of the Afghan Jihad and the Taliban
Sayyed Mohammad Akbar Agha

Following in the tradition of Mullah Zaeef's My Life With the Taliban, Akbar Agha's memoir tells a story of war, friendship and political intrigue. Starting in 1980s Kandahar, the difficulties and successes of the mujahedeen come through clearly as Akbar Agha struggles to administer a group of fighters. He details the different groups fighting in Kandahar, their cooperation and the scale of the Soviet Union's efforts to crush them. Not directly a participant in the Taliban gov-

ernment that ruled post-1994, Akbar Agha offers a some-
times-critical account of the administration built by many of
his former fighters. After the fall of the Islamic Emirate in
2001, Akbar Agha was involved in the Jaish ul-Muslimeen
opposition group and for the first time he has revealed his
account of what happened in the kidnapping of UN aid
workers. I Am Akbar Agha ends with an analysis of the problems afflicting Afghanistan and outlines a vision for the political future of the country post-elections and post-2015.
Anand Gopal has written an introduction to the book.

"Mandatory reading"
— Graeme Smith, Senior Analyst for Afghanistan

Kandahar Assassins: Stories from the Afghan-Soviet War
Mohammad Tahir Aziz Gumnam

Assassinations are a near-daily occurrence in Afghanistan. Whether by rogue Afghan security forces or by lone individuals roaming the cities and districts, the threat of a target killing is very real. Kandahar Assassins offers an unparalleled view of this phenomenon from the perspective of the assassins. Published in 1986 in Pashto and a perennial classic in Kandahar's bookstores, Kandahar Assassins tells the story of two well-known assassins who operated in the southern city during the 1980s war. The stories of 'Lame Ghazi' and Commander Ghaffari involve ambitious raids and plots carried out within the Afghan-controlled city. This book offers a corrective to the idea that assassination is a new phenomenon in Afghanistan. Mohammad Tahir Aziz Gumnam was a doctor working in Pakistan at the time, allowing him access to a variety of figures within the Afghan mujahedeen. Originally from Kandahar, Gumnam offers insight as an Afghan who was close to both the events and the people he describes. Judging from this book, the style and manner of assassinations in southern Afghanistan doesn't appear to have changed much. Kandahar Assassins, therefore, offers a unique perspective on the world of these target killers and how they carry out their operations. It is an essential read for any soldier serving in Afghanistan as well as those seeking to understand the history behind the current conflict. Dr David Kilcullen wrote the introduction to this English translation of the book.

"a Thousand-and-One Nights of the Afghan jihad... a detailed and lyrical account of the war that he and his contemporaries fought against in Kandahar during the 1980s"

— Dr David Kilcullen (from his introduction), counterinsurgency expert and author

An Undesirable Element: An Afghan Memoir
Dr Sharif Fayez

This is the incredible story of a relentless educator named
Sharif Fayez, born in 1946 in Herat, Afghanistan, who bore
witness to the Communist invasion of 1979, the Iranian revolution of 1979, and who authored a ground breaking PhD
dissertation that forever linked the best American poetry to
Afghanistan by proving that Walt Whitman had read and
been inspired by Rumi. It is the story of how Sharif pursues
education above all else and becomes a professor at Kabul
University only to flee illegally to Iran when the Soviets in-
vade, where he becomes caught in the violent Islamic revolution as a professor at Mashad University. Surviving the
Afghan and Iranian governments' ruthless campaign to silence academics and their students, as well as the Iran-Iraq
War, he becomes a prominent voice of resistance against the
Taliban and extremism in the 1990s, writing hundreds of ar-
ticles, and ultimately returns to Afghanistan as a signatory to
the 2001 Bonn Conference and as the Minister of Higher
Education. He completely overhauls the Afghan education
system, restores co-education to the country and establishes
six new universities. He is almost single-handedly responsible for the incredible strides the Afghan education system
has made since 2002.

"An Undesirable Element is a fascinating tour through the tumultuous years that helped create modern Afghanistan. Fayez survived Soviet Afghanistan and revolutionary Iran, only to find himself watching from exile as his country devoured itself. Improbably, he returns after 2001 to help resurrect Afghanistan's devastated higher education system, giving an insider account of the challenges of building education in a land dominated by warlords and fundamentalism. The result is a poignant reminder of how much Afghanistan has endured, and the flicker of hope that remains despite it all."

— Anand Gopal, author of *No Good Men Among The Living*

"A compelling read, An Undesirable Element recounts an Afghanistan many have forgotten. It serves as a rallying cry to once again imagine all that country might be. It's a tale as extraordinary as the land from which it comes."

— Elliot Ackerman, author of *Green On Blue*

"An Undesirable Element moves fast as flames and offers a luminous account of the last half century of Afghan conflicts and redevelopment. Trevithick's oral history of Sharif Fayez's story is a trove: from a kiss on the head by the Afghan former King Zahir Shah, Fayez's life intersected with the future leaders and quiet supporters of his country—both heroic and tyrannical— from Columbia University to a Post-revolutionary University in Mashad, Iran. Fayez is a modest but robust storyteller whose eventual position as Afghanistan's first Minister of Education after the Taliban is only one of the strange twists and turns his story offers. His deft handling in the rebuilding of Afghanistan should be read by anyone interested in how one can use patience and determination to bring hope to a country reduced to rubble."

— Adam Klein, editor, *The Gifts of The State: New Afghan Writing*

"The term visionary tends to be misapplied to those who are merely headstrong. But it is a perfectly apt description for Sharif Fayez, the most important figure in education in 21st-century Afghanistan, yet one that history may have neglected without his memoir. Such an omission would have deprived future generations of Afghans from understanding how Fayez, perhaps more than any single person, created hope for the country's young minds at the turn of the millennium and, in so doing, altered a nation's destiny."

— Martin Kuz, Freelance journalist

First Draft Publishing/*Primary*

Mufti Rasheed Ludhianvi: Obedience to the Amir
An Early Text on the Afghan Taliban Movement
Sample and Misha: Commentary and Translation

Obedience to the Amir: An early Text on the Afghan Taliban Movement
Mufti Rasheed Ludhianvi

In the last year of the Taliban's government in Afghanistan, visitors to Mullah Omar's office in Kandahar received a parting gift. As they left, the movement's supreme leader asked them to take a slim volume from a pile beside the door. He told them that if they wanted to know how the Taliban were meant to behave, they should read the book. The books which Mullah Omar handed out were Pashto and Farsi translation of *Eta't Amir*, or 'Obedience to the Leader'. Mufti Rasheed published the original in Urdu after having toured Taliban-run Afghanistan. Mullah Omar's endorsement indicates that he believed that Rasheed had captured the essence of the Taliban Movement. Michael Semple and Yameema Mitha have translated this important primary source and added a commentary and appraisal.

"In war, and especially guerrilla war, the best organised party is likely to win. While numbers of fighters and weapons count, organisation determines whether the leader can use them. This book is the guide the Afghan Taliban used to organise themselves differently from other Afghan groups. Anyone who wants

to defeat them or negotiate with them should understand the organisational principles that guide them."

— Barnett R. Rubin, Center on International Cooperation, New York University.

Taliban: A Critical History from Within
Abdul Hai Mutma'in

Taliban: A Critical History from Within by Abdul Hai Mutma'in offers an inside account of the Afghan movement and their government. In his preface, the author notes that his book will please neither supporters of the Taliban nor those who fight and condemn them. It is this trenchant quality that makes it unique among the memoirs of those who used to work for and with the Taliban. Mutma'in's account often feels like a corrective, critical of those outside the Taliban but also of the movement itself. Whereas most books of this kind stop with the invasion of the United States in October 2001, Mutma'in shares the story of how the Taliban fled, how resistance was organised and how they grew into a potent insurgency force. Mutma'in's book is essential reading for anyone seeking to understand the Taliban and recent Afghan history.

Delivering Osama: The Story of America's
Secret Envoy
Kabir Mohabbat and Leah McInnis

I, M. Kabir Mohabbat, acted as a secret diplomatic envoy
from the United States Government to the government of
the Taliban in Afghanistan. My first trip was in June 1999. My
last trip began on September 5, 2001. The purpose of the
trips eventually became to arrange for the delivery of Osama
bin Laden into the hands of the United States using diplomatic channels. I was successful. Towards the end of February
2001, the Taliban put bin Laden under house arrest for the
U.S. So why didn't we act? After September 11, 2001, I helped
negotiate the capitulation of the stubborn Afghan Government to U.S. demands. This is a narrative of my attempts to
secure Osama bin laden for the U.S., but it is also an insider's
look at the reclusive Taliban

Lightning Source UK Ltd.
Milton Keynes UK
UKHW020747160522
403010UK00009B/122